ISBN 0-8373-0142-4

C-142   CAREER EXAMINATION SERIES

W9-AXE-763

This is your
PASSBOOK® for...

Clerk

Test Preparation Study Guide

Questions & Answers

NATIONAL LEARNING CORPORATION

PASSBOOK® SERIES

THE *PASSBOOK® SERIES* has been created to prepare applicants and candidates for the ultimate academic battlefield — the examination room.

At some time in our lives, each and every one of us may be required to take an examination — for validation, matriculation, admission, qualification, registration, certification, or licensure.

Based on the assumption that every applicant or candidate has met the basic formal educational standards, has taken the required number of courses, and read the necessary texts, the *PASSBOOK® SERIES* furnishes the one special preparation which may assure passing with confidence, instead of failing with insecurity. Examination questions — together with answers — are furnished as the basic vehicle for study so that the mysteries of the examination and its compounding difficulties may be eliminated or diminished by a sure method.

This book is meant to help you pass your examination provided that you qualify and are serious in your objective.

The entire field is reviewed through the huge store of content information which is succinctly presented through a provocative and challenging approach — the question-and-answer method.

A climate of success is established by furnishing the correct answers at the end of each test.

You soon learn to recognize types of questions, forms of questions, and patterns of questioning. You may even begin to anticipate expected outcomes.

You perceive that many questions are repeated or adapted so that you can gain acute insights, which may enable you to score many sure points.

You learn how to confront new questions, or types of questions, and to attack them confidently and work out the correct answers.

You note objectives and emphases, and recognize pitfalls and dangers, so that you may make positive educational adjustments.

Moreover, you are kept fully informed in relation to new concepts, methods, practices, and directions in the field.

You discover that you are actually taking the examination all the time: you are preparing for the examination by "taking" an examination, not by reading extraneous and/or supererogatory textbooks.

In short, this PASSBOOK®, used directedly, should be an important factor in helping you to pass your test.

CLERK

DUTIES

Under general supervision, this position performs general clerical work of ordinary difficulty and related duties as required. Essential functions include: alphabetical, numerical and/or chronological filing; examining, sorting, indexing, coding and reviewing documents for completeness and accuracy; performing a variety of mathematical computations; operating various types of office equipment; processing and distributing mail; responsibility for explaining and carrying out existing methods and procedures relative to office operations; making routine contacts with other departmental employees and the general public in connection with office operations; and gathering, preparing and maintaining a wide variety of records and reports of some complexity.

EXAMPLES OF WORK

Reviews documents for accuracy and completeness according to procedures and instructions; sorts large volume production work such as applications and various printed material and official documents into sets of predetermined arrangement and number and assigns sequential numbers to each set; prepares folders on individual program cases with appropriate documentation per established system; issues notification to affected individuals on specific agency program actions per established procedures; codes various transactions for computer input from source documents per established coding system; checks arithmetic accuracy of certain calculations; posts receipt of payments for various routine program activities to individual accounts; compares computer printouts with other records for discrepancies, checks source documents to identify cause of error and notes appropriate corrective action for supervisor; obtains and confirms routine data by telephone or form letter and posts results; uses a data entry terminal keyboard and a visual screen to enter and retrieve pertinent data from computer files; logs receipt of various documents, applications and forms; alphabetizes folders and other records; answers routine factual telephone inquiries and/or refers callers to appropriate office of individual; makes entries on control cards from original sources; answers questions from individual members of the public while performing work at a counter or information station; types correspondence, records and other written materials.

SCOPE OF THE EXAMINATION

The written test will cover knowledge, skills and/or abilities in such areas as:
1. Clerical abilities and operations;
2. Name and number checking;
3. Record keeping;
4. Arithmetic computations;
5. English usage (spelling, punctuation, capitalization);
6. Reading comprehension; and
7. Office practices.

HOW TO TAKE A TEST

I. YOU MUST PASS AN EXAMINATION

A. *WHAT EVERY CANDIDATE SHOULD KNOW*

Examination applicants often ask us for help in preparing for the written test. What can I study in advance? What kinds of questions will be asked? How will the test be given? How will the papers be graded?

As an applicant for a civil service examination, you may be wondering about some of these things. Our purpose here is to suggest effective methods of advance study and to describe civil service examinations.

Your chances for success on this examination can be increased if you know how to prepare. Those "pre-examination jitters" can be reduced if you know what to expect. You can even experience an adventure in good citizenship if you know why civil service exams are given.

B. *WHY ARE CIVIL SERVICE EXAMINATIONS GIVEN?*

Civil service examinations are important to you in two ways. As a citizen, you want public jobs filled by employees who know how to do their work. As a job seeker, you want a fair chance to compete for that job on an equal footing with other candidates. The best-known means of accomplishing this two-fold goal is the competitive examination.

Exams are widely publicized throughout the nation. They may be administered for jobs in federal, state, city, municipal, town or village governments or agencies.

Any citizen may apply, with some limitations, such as the age or residence of applicants. Your experience and education may be reviewed to see whether you meet the requirements for the particular examination. When these requirements exist, they are reasonable and applied consistently to all applicants. Thus, a competitive examination may cause you some uneasiness now, but it is your privilege and safeguard.

C. *HOW ARE CIVIL SERVICE EXAMS DEVELOPED?*

Examinations are carefully written by trained technicians who are specialists in the field known as "psychological measurement," in consultation with recognized authorities in the field of work that the test will cover. These experts recommend the subject matter areas or skills to be tested; only those knowledges or skills important to your success on the job are included. The most reliable books and source materials available are used as references. Together, the experts and technicians judge the difficulty level of the questions.

Test technicians know how to phrase questions so that the problem is clearly stated. Their ethics do not permit "trick" or "catch" questions. Questions may have been tried out on sample groups, or subjected to statistical analysis, to determine their usefulness.

Written tests are often used in combination with performance tests, ratings of training and experience, and oral interviews. All of these measures combine to form the best-known means of finding the right person for the right job.

II. HOW TO PASS THE WRITTEN TEST

A. NATURE OF THE EXAMINATION

To prepare intelligently for civil service examinations, you should know how they differ from school examinations you have taken. In school you were assigned certain definite pages to read or subjects to cover. The examination questions were quite detailed and usually emphasized memory. Civil service exams, on the other hand, try to discover your present ability to perform the duties of a position, plus your potentiality to learn these duties. In other words, a civil service exam attempts to predict how successful you will be. Questions cover such a broad area that they cannot be as minute and detailed as school exam questions.

In the public service similar kinds of work, or positions, are grouped together in one "class." This process is known as *position-classification*. All the positions in a class are paid according to the salary range for that class. One class title covers all of these positions, and they are all tested by the same examination.

B. FOUR BASIC STEPS

1) Study the announcement

How, then, can you know what subjects to study? Our best answer is: "Learn as much as possible about the class of positions for which you've applied." The exam will test the knowledge, skills and abilities needed to do the work.

Your most valuable source of information about the position you want is the official exam announcement. This announcement lists the training and experience qualifications. Check these standards and apply only if you come reasonably close to meeting them.

The brief description of the position in the examination announcement offers some clues to the subjects which will be tested. Think about the job itself. Review the duties in your mind. Can you perform them, or are there some in which you are rusty? Fill in the blank spots in your preparation.

Many jurisdictions preview the written test in the exam announcement by including a section called "Knowledge and Abilities Required," "Scope of the Examination," or some similar heading. Here you will find out specifically what fields will be tested.

2) Review your own background

Once you learn in general what the position is all about, and what you need to know to do the work, ask yourself which subjects you already know fairly well and which need improvement. You may wonder whether to concentrate on improving your strong areas or on building some background in your fields of weakness. When the announcement has specified "some knowledge" or "considerable knowledge," or has used adjectives like "beginning principles of…" or "advanced … methods," you can get a clue as to the number and difficulty of questions to be asked in any given field. More questions, and hence broader coverage, would be included for those subjects which are more important in the work. Now weigh your strengths and weaknesses against the job requirements and prepare accordingly.

3) Determine the level of the position

Another way to tell how intensively you should prepare is to understand the level of the job for which you are applying. Is it the entering level? In other words, is this the position in which beginners in a field of work are hired? Or is it an intermediate or advanced level? Sometimes this is indicated by such words as "Junior" or "Senior" in the class title. Other jurisdictions use Roman numerals to designate the level – Clerk I, Clerk II, for example. The word "Supervisor" sometimes appears in the title. If the level is not indicated by the title, check the description of duties. Will you be working under very close supervision, or will you have responsibility for independent decisions in this work?

4) Choose appropriate study materials

Now that you know the subjects to be examined and the relative amount of each subject to be covered, you can choose suitable study materials. For beginning level jobs, or even advanced ones, if you have a pronounced weakness in some aspect of your training, read a modern, standard textbook in that field. Be sure it is up to date and has general coverage. Such books are normally available at your library, and the librarian will be glad to help you locate one. For entry-level positions, questions of appropriate difficulty are chosen – neither highly advanced questions, nor those too simple. Such questions require careful thought but not advanced training.

If the position for which you are applying is technical or advanced, you will read more advanced, specialized material. If you are already familiar with the basic principles of your field, elementary textbooks would waste your time. Concentrate on advanced textbooks and technical periodicals. Think through the concepts and review difficult problems in your field.

These are all general sources. You can get more ideas on your own initiative, following these leads. For example, training manuals and publications of the government agency which employs workers in your field can be useful, particularly for technical and professional positions. A letter or visit to the government department involved may result in more specific study suggestions, and certainly will provide you with a more definite idea of the exact nature of the position you are seeking.

III. KINDS OF TESTS

Tests are used for purposes other than measuring knowledge and ability to perform specified duties. For some positions, it is equally important to test ability to make adjustments to new situations or to profit from training. In others, basic mental abilities not dependent on information are essential. Questions which test these things may not appear as pertinent to the duties of the position as those which test for knowledge and information. Yet they are often highly important parts of a fair examination. For very general questions, it is almost impossible to help you direct your study efforts. What we can do is to point out some of the more common of these general abilities needed in public service positions and describe some typical questions.

1) General information

Broad, general information has been found useful for predicting job success in some kinds of work. This is tested in a variety of ways, from vocabulary lists to questions about current events. Basic background in some field of work, such as sociology or economics, may be sampled in a group of questions. Often these are principles which have become familiar to most persons through exposure rather than through formal training. It is difficult to advise you how to study for these questions; being alert to the world around you is our best suggestion.

2) Verbal ability

An example of an ability needed in many positions is verbal or language ability. Verbal ability is, in brief, the ability to use and understand words. Vocabulary and grammar tests are typical measures of this ability. Reading comprehension or paragraph interpretation questions are common in many kinds of civil service tests. You are given a paragraph of written material and asked to find its central meaning.

3) Numerical ability

Number skills can be tested by the familiar arithmetic problem, by checking paired lists of numbers to see which are alike and which are different, or by interpreting charts and graphs. In the latter test, a graph may be printed in the test booklet which you are asked to use as the basis for answering questions.

4) Observation

A popular test for law-enforcement positions is the observation test. A picture is shown to you for several minutes, then taken away. Questions about the picture test your ability to observe both details and larger elements.

5) Following directions

In many positions in the public service, the employee must be able to carry out written instructions dependably and accurately. You may be given a chart with several columns, each column listing a variety of information. The questions require you to carry out directions involving the information given in the chart.

6) Skills and aptitudes

Performance tests effectively measure some manual skills and aptitudes. When the skill is one in which you are trained, such as typing or shorthand, you can practice. These tests are often very much like those given in business school or high school courses. For many of the other skills and aptitudes, however, no short-time preparation can be made. Skills and abilities natural to you or that you have developed throughout your lifetime are being tested.

Many of the general questions just described provide all the data needed to answer the questions and ask you to use your reasoning ability to find the answers. Your best preparation for these tests, as well as for tests of facts and ideas, is to be at your physical and mental best. You, no doubt, have your own methods of getting into an exam-taking mood and keeping "in shape." The next section lists some ideas on this subject.

IV. KINDS OF QUESTIONS

Only rarely is the "essay" question, which you answer in narrative form, used in civil service tests. Civil service tests are usually of the short-answer type. Full instructions for answering these questions will be given to you at the examination. But in case this is your first experience with short-answer questions and separate answer sheets, here is what you need to know:

1) Multiple-choice Questions

Most popular of the short-answer questions is the "multiple choice" or "best answer" question. It can be used, for example, to test for factual knowledge, ability to solve problems or judgment in meeting situations found at work.

A multiple-choice question is normally one of three types—

- It can begin with an incomplete statement followed by several possible endings. You are to find the one ending which *best* completes the statement, although some of the others may not be entirely wrong.
- It can also be a complete statement in the form of a question which is answered by choosing one of the statements listed.

- It can be in the form of a problem – again you select the best answer.

Here is an example of a multiple-choice question with a discussion which should give you some clues as to the method for choosing the right answer:

When an employee has a complaint about his assignment, the action which will *best* help him overcome his difficulty is to
- A. discuss his difficulty with his coworkers
- B. take the problem to the head of the organization
- C. take the problem to the person who gave him the assignment
- D. say nothing to anyone about his complaint

In answering this question, you should study each of the choices to find which is best. Consider choice "A" – Certainly an employee may discuss his complaint with fellow employees, but no change or improvement can result, and the complaint remains unresolved. Choice "B" is a poor choice since the head of the organization probably does not know what assignment you have been given, and taking your problem to him is known as "going over the head" of the supervisor. The supervisor, or person who made the assignment, is the person who can clarify it or correct any injustice. Choice "C" is, therefore, correct. To say nothing, as in choice "D," is unwise. Supervisors have and interest in knowing the problems employees are facing, and the employee is seeking a solution to his problem.

2) True/False Questions

The "true/false" or "right/wrong" form of question is sometimes used. Here a complete statement is given. Your job is to decide whether the statement is right or wrong.

SAMPLE: A roaming cell-phone call to a nearby city costs less than a non-roaming call to a distant city.

This statement is wrong, or false, since roaming calls are more expensive.

This is not a complete list of all possible question forms, although most of the others are variations of these common types. You will always get complete directions for answering questions. Be sure you understand *how* to mark your answers – ask questions until you do.

V. RECORDING YOUR ANSWERS

Computer terminals are used more and more today for many different kinds of exams.

For an examination with very few applicants, you may be told to record your answers in the test booklet itself. Separate answer sheets are much more common. If this separate answer sheet is to be scored by machine – and this is often the case – it is highly important that you mark your answers correctly in order to get credit.

An electronic scoring machine is often used in civil service offices because of the speed with which papers can be scored. Machine-scored answer sheets must be marked with a pencil, which will be given to you. This pencil has a high graphite content which responds to the electronic scoring machine. As a matter of fact, stray dots may register as answers, so do not let your pencil rest on the answer sheet while you are pondering the correct answer. Also, if your pencil lead breaks or is otherwise defective, ask for another.

Since the answer sheet will be dropped in a slot in the scoring machine, be careful not to bend the corners or get the paper crumpled.

The answer sheet normally has five vertical columns of numbers, with 30 numbers to a column. These numbers correspond to the question numbers in your test booklet. After each number, going across the page are four or five pairs of dotted lines. These short dotted lines have small letters or numbers above them. The first two pairs may also have a "T" or "F" above the letters. This indicates that the first two pairs only are to be used if the questions are of the true-false type. If the questions are multiple choice, disregard the "T" and "F" and pay attention only to the small letters or numbers.

Answer your questions in the manner of the sample that follows:

32. The largest city in the United States is
    A. Washington, D.C.
    B. New York City
    C. Chicago
    D. Detroit
    E. San Francisco

1) Choose the answer you think is best. (New York City is the largest, so "B" is correct.)
2) Find the row of dotted lines numbered the same as the question you are answering. (Find row number 32)
3) Find the pair of dotted lines corresponding to the answer. (Find the pair of lines under the mark "B.")
4) Make a solid black mark between the dotted lines.

VI. BEFORE THE TEST

Common sense will help you find procedures to follow to get ready for an examination. Too many of us, however, overlook these sensible measures. Indeed, nervousness and fatigue have been found to be the most serious reasons why applicants fail to do their best on civil service tests. Here is a list of reminders:

- Begin your preparation early – Don't wait until the last minute to go scurrying around for books and materials or to find out what the position is all about.
- Prepare continuously – An hour a night for a week is better than an all-night cram session. This has been definitely established. What is more, a night a week for a month will return better dividends than crowding your study into a shorter period of time.
- Locate the place of the exam – You have been sent a notice telling you when and where to report for the examination. If the location is in a different town or otherwise unfamiliar to you, it would be well to inquire the best route and learn something about the building.
- Relax the night before the test – Allow your mind to rest. Do not study at all that night. Plan some mild recreation or diversion; then go to bed early and get a good night's sleep.
- Get up early enough to make a leisurely trip to the place for the test – This way unforeseen events, traffic snarls, unfamiliar buildings, etc. will not upset you.
- Dress comfortably – A written test is not a fashion show. You will be known by number and not by name, so wear something comfortable.

- Leave excess paraphernalia at home – Shopping bags and odd bundles will get in your way. You need bring only the items mentioned in the official notice you received; usually everything you need is provided. Do not bring reference books to the exam. They will only confuse those last minutes and be taken away from you when in the test room.
- Arrive somewhat ahead of time – If because of transportation schedules you must get there very early, bring a newspaper or magazine to take your mind off yourself while waiting.
- Locate the examination room – When you have found the proper room, you will be directed to the seat or part of the room where you will sit. Sometimes you are given a sheet of instructions to read while you are waiting. Do not fill out any forms until you are told to do so; just read them and be prepared.
- Relax and prepare to listen to the instructions
- If you have any physical problem that may keep you from doing your best, be sure to tell the test administrator. If you are sick or in poor health, you really cannot do your best on the exam. You can come back and take the test some other time.

VII. AT THE TEST

The day of the test is here and you have the test booklet in your hand. The temptation to get going is very strong. Caution! There is more to success than knowing the right answers. You must know how to identify your papers and understand variations in the type of short-answer question used in this particular examination. Follow these suggestions for maximum results from your efforts:

1) Cooperate with the monitor
The test administrator has a duty to create a situation in which you can be as much at ease as possible. He will give instructions, tell you when to begin, check to see that you are marking your answer sheet correctly, and so on. He is not there to guard you, although he will see that your competitors do not take unfair advantage. He wants to help you do your best.

2) Listen to all instructions
Don't jump the gun! Wait until you understand all directions. In most civil service tests you get more time than you need to answer the questions. So don't be in a hurry. Read each word of instructions until you clearly understand the meaning. Study the examples, listen to all announcements and follow directions. Ask questions if you do not understand what to do.

3) Identify your papers
Civil service exams are usually identified by number only. You will be assigned a number; you must not put your name on your test papers. Be sure to copy your number correctly. Since more than one exam may be given, copy your exact examination title.

4) Plan your time
Unless you are told that a test is a "speed" or "rate of work" test, speed itself is usually not important. Time enough to answer all the questions will be provided, but this does not mean that you have all day. An overall time limit has been set. Divide the total time (in minutes) by the number of questions to determine the approximate time you have for each question.

5) Do not linger over difficult questions

If you come across a difficult question, mark it with a paper clip (useful to have along) and come back to it when you have been through the booklet. One caution if you do this – be sure to skip a number on your answer sheet as well. Check often to be sure that you have not lost your place and that you are marking in the row numbered the same as the question you are answering.

6) Read the questions

Be sure you know what the question asks! Many capable people are unsuccessful because they failed to *read* the questions correctly.

7) Answer all questions

Unless you have been instructed that a penalty will be deducted for incorrect answers, it is better to guess than to omit a question.

8) Speed tests

It is often better NOT to guess on speed tests. It has been found that on timed tests people are tempted to spend the last few seconds before time is called in marking answers at random – without even reading them – in the hope of picking up a few extra points. To discourage this practice, the instructions may warn you that your score will be "corrected" for guessing. That is, a penalty will be applied. The incorrect answers will be deducted from the correct ones, or some other penalty formula will be used.

9) Review your answers

If you finish before time is called, go back to the questions you guessed or omitted to give them further thought. Review other answers if you have time.

10) Return your test materials

If you are ready to leave before others have finished or time is called, take ALL your materials to the monitor and leave quietly. Never take any test material with you. The monitor can discover whose papers are not complete, and taking a test booklet may be grounds for disqualification.

VIII. EXAMINATION TECHNIQUES

1) Read the general instructions carefully. These are usually printed on the first page of the exam booklet. As a rule, these instructions refer to the timing of the examination; the fact that you should not start work until the signal and must stop work at a signal, etc. If there are any *special* instructions, such as a choice of questions to be answered, make sure that you note this instruction carefully.

2) When you are ready to start work on the examination, that is as soon as the signal has been given, read the instructions to each question booklet, underline any key words or phrases, such as *least*, *best*, *outline*, *describe* and the like. In this way you will tend to answer as requested rather than discover on reviewing your paper that you *listed without describing*, that you selected the *worst* choice rather than the *best* choice, etc.

3) If the examination is of the objective or multiple-choice type – that is, each question will also give a series of possible answers: A, B, C or D, and you are called upon to select the best answer and write the letter next to that answer on your answer paper – it is advisable to start answering each question in turn. There may be anywhere from 50 to 100 such questions in the three or four hours allotted and you can see how much time would be taken if you read through all the questions before beginning to answer any. Furthermore, if you come across a question or group of questions which you know would be difficult to answer, it would undoubtedly affect your handling of all the other questions.

4) If the examination is of the essay type and contains but a few questions, it is a moot point as to whether you should read all the questions before starting to answer any one. Of course, if you are given a choice – say five out of seven and the like – then it is essential to read all the questions so you can eliminate the two that are most difficult. If, however, you are asked to answer all the questions, there may be danger in trying to answer the easiest one first because you may find that you will spend too much time on it. The best technique is to answer the first question, then proceed to the second, etc.

5) Time your answers. Before the exam begins, write down the time it started, then add the time allowed for the examination and write down the time it must be completed, then divide the time available somewhat as follows:
   - If 3-1/2 hours are allowed, that would be 210 minutes. If you have 80 objective-type questions, that would be an average of 2-1/2 minutes per question. Allow yourself no more than 2 minutes per question, or a total of 160 minutes, which will permit about 50 minutes to review.
   - If for the time allotment of 210 minutes there are 7 essay questions to answer, that would average about 30 minutes a question. Give yourself only 25 minutes per question so that you have about 35 minutes to review.

6) The most important instruction is to *read each question* and make sure you know what is wanted. The second most important instruction is to *time yourself properly* so that you answer every question. The third most important instruction is to *answer every question*. Guess if you have to but include something for each question. Remember that you will receive no credit for a blank and will probably receive some credit if you write something in answer to an essay question. If you guess a letter – say "B" for a multiple-choice question – you may have guessed right. If you leave a blank as an answer to a multiple-choice question, the examiners may respect your feelings but it will not add a point to your score. Some exams may penalize you for wrong answers, so in such cases *only*, you may not want to guess unless you have some basis for your answer.

7) Suggestions
   a. Objective-type questions
      1. Examine the question booklet for proper sequence of pages and questions
      2. Read all instructions carefully
      3. Skip any question which seems too difficult; return to it after all other questions have been answered
      4. Apportion your time properly; do not spend too much time on any single question or group of questions

5. Note and underline key words – *all, most, fewest, least, best, worst, same, opposite,* etc.
6. Pay particular attention to negatives
7. Note unusual option, e.g., unduly long, short, complex, different or similar in content to the body of the question
8. Observe the use of "hedging" words – *probably, may, most likely,* etc.
9. Make sure that your answer is put next to the same number as the question
10. Do not second-guess unless you have good reason to believe the second answer is definitely more correct
11. Cross out original answer if you decide another answer is more accurate; do not erase until you are ready to hand your paper in
12. Answer all questions; guess unless instructed otherwise
13. Leave time for review

b. Essay questions
1. Read each question carefully
2. Determine exactly what is wanted. Underline key words or phrases.
3. Decide on outline or paragraph answer
4. Include many different points and elements unless asked to develop any one or two points or elements
5. Show impartiality by giving pros and cons unless directed to select one side only
6. Make and write down any assumptions you find necessary to answer the questions
7. Watch your English, grammar, punctuation and choice of words
8. Time your answers; don't crowd material

8) Answering the essay question

Most essay questions can be answered by framing the specific response around several key words or ideas. Here are a few such key words or ideas:

M's: manpower, materials, methods, money, management
P's: purpose, program, policy, plan, procedure, practice, problems, pitfalls, personnel, public relations
a. Six basic steps in handling problems:
1. Preliminary plan and background development
2. Collect information, data and facts
3. Analyze and interpret information, data and facts
4. Analyze and develop solutions as well as make recommendations
5. Prepare report and sell recommendations
6. Install recommendations and follow up effectiveness

b. Pitfalls to avoid
1. *Taking things for granted* – A statement of the situation does not necessarily imply that each of the elements is necessarily true; for example, a complaint may be invalid and biased so that all that can be taken for granted is that a complaint has been registered

2. *Considering only one side of a situation* – Wherever possible, indicate several alternatives and then point out the reasons you selected the best one
3. *Failing to indicate follow up* – Whenever your answer indicates action on your part, make certain that you will take proper follow-up action to see how successful your recommendations, procedures or actions turn out to be
4. *Taking too long in answering any single question* – Remember to time your answers properly

IX. AFTER THE TEST

Scoring procedures differ in detail among civil service jurisdictions although the general principles are the same. Whether the papers are hand-scored or graded by machine we have described, they are nearly always graded by number. That is, the person who marks the paper knows only the number – never the name – of the applicant. Not until all the papers have been graded will they be matched with names. If other tests, such as training and experience or oral interview ratings have been given, scores will be combined. Different parts of the examination usually have different weights. For example, the written test might count 60 percent of the final grade, and a rating of training and experience 40 percent. In many jurisdictions, veterans will have a certain number of points added to their grades.

After the final grade has been determined, the names are placed in grade order and an eligible list is established. There are various methods for resolving ties between those who get the same final grade – probably the most common is to place first the name of the person whose application was received first. Job offers are made from the eligible list in the order the names appear on it. You will be notified of your grade and your rank as soon as all these computations have been made. This will be done as rapidly as possible.

People who are found to meet the requirements in the announcement are called "eligibles." Their names are put on a list of eligible candidates. An eligible's chances of getting a job depend on how high he stands on this list and how fast agencies are filling jobs from the list.

When a job is to be filled from a list of eligibles, the agency asks for the names of people on the list of eligibles for that job. When the civil service commission receives this request, it sends to the agency the names of the three people highest on this list. Or, if the job to be filled has specialized requirements, the office sends the agency the names of the top three persons who meet these requirements from the general list.

The appointing officer makes a choice from among the three people whose names were sent to him. If the selected person accepts the appointment, the names of the others are put back on the list to be considered for future openings.

That is the rule in hiring from all kinds of eligible lists, whether they are for typist, carpenter, chemist, or something else. For every vacancy, the appointing officer has his choice of any one of the top three eligibles on the list. This explains why the person whose name is on top of the list sometimes does not get an appointment when some of the persons lower on the list do. If the appointing officer chooses the second or third eligible, the No. 1 eligible does not get a job at once, but stays on the list until he is appointed or the list is terminated.

X. HOW TO PASS THE INTERVIEW TEST

The examination for which you applied requires an oral interview test. You have already taken the written test and you are now being called for the interview test – the final part of the formal examination.

You may think that it is not possible to prepare for an interview test and that there are no procedures to follow during an interview. Our purpose is to point out some things you can do in advance that will help you and some good rules to follow and pitfalls to avoid while you are being interviewed.

What is an interview supposed to test?

The written examination is designed to test the technical knowledge and competence of the candidate; the oral is designed to evaluate intangible qualities, not readily measured otherwise, and to establish a list showing the relative fitness of each candidate – as measured against his competitors – for the position sought. Scoring is not on the basis of "right" and "wrong," but on a sliding scale of values ranging from "not passable" to "outstanding." As a matter of fact, it is possible to achieve a relatively low score without a single "incorrect" answer because of evident weakness in the qualities being measured.

Occasionally, an examination may consist entirely of an oral test – either an individual or a group oral. In such cases, information is sought concerning the technical knowledges and abilities of the candidate, since there has been no written examination for this purpose. More commonly, however, an oral test is used to supplement a written examination.

Who conducts interviews?

The composition of oral boards varies among different jurisdictions. In nearly all, a representative of the personnel department serves as chairman. One of the members of the board may be a representative of the department in which the candidate would work. In some cases, "outside experts" are used, and, frequently, a businessman or some other representative of the general public is asked to serve. Labor and management or other special groups may be represented. The aim is to secure the services of experts in the appropriate field.

However the board is composed, it is a good idea (and not at all improper or unethical) to ascertain in advance of the interview who the members are and what groups they represent. When you are introduced to them, you will have some idea of their backgrounds and interests, and at least you will not stutter and stammer over their names.

What should be done before the interview?

While knowledge about the board members is useful and takes some of the surprise element out of the interview, there is other preparation which is more substantive. It *is* possible to prepare for an oral interview – in several ways:

1) Keep a copy of your application and review it carefully before the interview

This may be the only document before the oral board, and the starting point of the interview. Know what education and experience you have listed there, and the sequence and dates of all of it. Sometimes the board will ask you to review the highlights of your experience for them; you should not have to hem and haw doing it.

2) Study the class specification and the examination announcement

Usually, the oral board has one or both of these to guide them. The qualities, characteristics or knowledges required by the position sought are stated in these documents. They offer valuable clues as to the nature of the oral interview. For example, if the job involves supervisory responsibilities, the announcement will usually indicate that knowledge of modern supervisory methods and the qualifications of the candidate as a supervisor will be tested. If so, you can expect such questions, frequently in the form of a hypothetical situation which you are expected to solve. NEVER go into an oral without knowledge of the duties and responsibilities of the job you seek.

3) Think through each qualification required

Try to visualize the kind of questions you would ask if you were a board member. How well could you answer them? Try especially to appraise your own knowledge and background in each area, *measured against the job sought*, and identify any areas in which you are weak. Be critical and realistic – do not flatter yourself.

4) Do some general reading in areas in which you feel you may be weak

For example, if the job involves supervision and your past experience has NOT, some general reading in supervisory methods and practices, particularly in the field of human relations, might be useful. Do NOT study agency procedures or detailed manuals. The oral board will be testing your understanding and capacity, not your memory.

5) Get a good night's sleep and watch your general health and mental attitude

You will want a clear head at the interview. Take care of a cold or any other minor ailment, and of course, no hangovers.

What should be done on the day of the interview?

Now comes the day of the interview itself. Give yourself plenty of time to get there. Plan to arrive somewhat ahead of the scheduled time, particularly if your appointment is in the fore part of the day. If a previous candidate fails to appear, the board might be ready for you a bit early. By early afternoon an oral board is almost invariably behind schedule if there are many candidates, and you may have to wait. Take along a book or magazine to read, or your application to review, but leave any extraneous material in the waiting room when you go in for your interview. In any event, relax and compose yourself.

The matter of dress is important. The board is forming impressions about you – from your experience, your manners, your attitude, and your appearance. Give your personal appearance careful attention. Dress your best, but not your flashiest. Choose conservative, appropriate clothing, and be sure it is immaculate. This is a business interview, and your appearance should indicate that you regard it as such. Besides, being well groomed and properly dressed will help boost your confidence.

Sooner or later, someone will call your name and escort you into the interview room. *This is it.* From here on you are on your own. It is too late for any more preparation. But remember, you asked for this opportunity to prove your fitness, and you are here because your request was granted.

What happens when you go in?

The usual sequence of events will be as follows: The clerk (who is often the board stenographer) will introduce you to the chairman of the oral board, who will introduce you to the other members of the board. Acknowledge the introductions before you sit down. Do not be surprised if you find a microphone facing you or a stenotypist sitting by. Oral interviews are usually recorded in the event of an appeal or other review.

Usually the chairman of the board will open the interview by reviewing the highlights of your education and work experience from your application – primarily for the benefit of the other members of the board, as well as to get the material into the record. Do not interrupt or comment unless there is an error or significant misinterpretation; if that is the case, do not hesitate. But do not quibble about insignificant matters. Also, he will usually ask you some question about your education, experience or your present job – partly to get you to start talking and to establish the interviewing "rapport." He may start the actual questioning, or turn it over to one of the other members. Frequently, each member undertakes the questioning on a particular area, one in which he is perhaps most competent, so you can expect each member to participate in the examination. Because time is limited, you may also expect some rather abrupt switches in the direction the questioning takes, so do not be upset by it. Normally, a board member will not pursue a single line of questioning unless he discovers a particular strength or weakness.

After each member has participated, the chairman will usually ask whether any member has any further questions, then will ask you if you have anything you wish to add. Unless you are expecting this question, it may floor you. Worse, it may start you off on an extended, extemporaneous speech. The board is not usually seeking more information. The question is principally to offer you a last opportunity to present further qualifications or to indicate that you have nothing to add. So, if you feel that a significant qualification or characteristic has been overlooked, it is proper to point it out in a sentence or so. Do not compliment the board on the thoroughness of their examination – they have been sketchy, and you know it. If you wish, merely say, "No thank you, I have nothing further to add." This is a point where you can "talk yourself out" of a good impression or fail to present an important bit of information. Remember, *you close the interview yourself.*

The chairman will then say, "That is all, Mr. _____, thank you." Do not be startled; the interview is over, and quicker than you think. Thank him, gather your belongings and take your leave. Save your sigh of relief for the other side of the door.

How to put your best foot forward

Throughout this entire process, you may feel that the board individually and collectively is trying to pierce your defenses, seek out your hidden weaknesses and embarrass and confuse you. Actually, this is not true. They are obliged to make an appraisal of your qualifications for the job you are seeking, and they want to see you in your best light. Remember, they must interview all candidates and a non-cooperative candidate may become a failure in spite of their best efforts to bring out his qualifications. Here are 15 suggestions that will help you:

1) Be natural – Keep your attitude confident, not cocky

If you are not confident that you can do the job, do not expect the board to be. Do not apologize for your weaknesses, try to bring out your strong points. The board is interested in a positive, not negative, presentation. Cockiness will antagonize any board member and make him wonder if you are covering up a weakness by a false show of strength.

2) Get comfortable, but don't lounge or sprawl

Sit erectly but not stiffly. A careless posture may lead the board to conclude that you are careless in other things, or at least that you are not impressed by the importance of the occasion. Either conclusion is natural, even if incorrect. Do not fuss with your clothing, a pencil or an ashtray. Your hands may occasionally be useful to emphasize a point; do not let them become a point of distraction.

3) Do not wisecrack or make small talk

This is a serious situation, and your attitude should show that you consider it as such. Further, the time of the board is limited – they do not want to waste it, and neither should you.

4) Do not exaggerate your experience or abilities

In the first place, from information in the application or other interviews and sources, the board may know more about you than you think. Secondly, you probably will not get away with it. An experienced board is rather adept at spotting such a situation, so do not take the chance.

5) If you know a board member, do not make a point of it, yet do not hide it

Certainly you are not fooling him, and probably not the other members of the board. Do not try to take advantage of your acquaintanceship – it will probably do you little good.

6) Do not dominate the interview

Let the board do that. They will give you the clues – do not assume that you have to do all the talking. Realize that the board has a number of questions to ask you, and do not try to take up all the interview time by showing off your extensive knowledge of the answer to the first one.

7) Be attentive

You only have 20 minutes or so, and you should keep your attention at its sharpest throughout. When a member is addressing a problem or question to you, give him your undivided attention. Address your reply principally to him, but do not exclude the other board members.

8) Do not interrupt

A board member may be stating a problem for you to analyze. He will ask you a question when the time comes. Let him state the problem, and wait for the question.

9) Make sure you understand the question

Do not try to answer until you are sure what the question is. If it is not clear, restate it in your own words or ask the board member to clarify it for you. However, do not haggle about minor elements.

10) Reply promptly but not hastily

A common entry on oral board rating sheets is "candidate responded readily," or "candidate hesitated in replies." Respond as promptly and quickly as you can, but do not jump to a hasty, ill-considered answer.

11) Do not be peremptory in your answers

A brief answer is proper – but do not fire your answer back. That is a losing game from your point of view. The board member can probably ask questions much faster than you can answer them.

12) Do not try to create the answer you think the board member wants

He is interested in what kind of mind you have and how it works – not in playing games. Furthermore, he can usually spot this practice and will actually grade you down on it.

13) Do not switch sides in your reply merely to agree with a board member

Frequently, a member will take a contrary position merely to draw you out and to see if you are willing and able to defend your point of view. Do not start a debate, yet do not surrender a good position. If a position is worth taking, it is worth defending.

14) Do not be afraid to admit an error in judgment if you are shown to be wrong

The board knows that you are forced to reply without any opportunity for careful consideration. Your answer may be demonstrably wrong. If so, admit it and get on with the interview.

15) Do not dwell at length on your present job

The opening question may relate to your present assignment. Answer the question but do not go into an extended discussion. You are being examined for a *new* job, not your present one. As a matter of fact, try to phrase ALL your answers in terms of the job for which you are being examined.

Basis of Rating

Probably you will forget most of these "do's" and "don'ts" when you walk into the oral interview room. Even remembering them all will not ensure you a passing grade. Perhaps you did not have the qualifications in the first place. But remembering them will help you to put your best foot forward, without treading on the toes of the board members.

Rumor and popular opinion to the contrary notwithstanding, an oral board wants you to make the best appearance possible. They know you are under pressure – but they also want to see how you respond to it as a guide to what your reaction would be under the pressures of the job you seek. They will be influenced by the degree of poise you display, the personal traits you show and the manner in which you respond.

ABOUT THIS BOOK

This book contains tests, divided into Examination Sections. Go through each test, answering every question in the margin. We have also attached a sample answer sheet at the back of the book that can be removed and used. At the end of each test look at the answer key and check your answers. On the ones you got wrong, look at the right answer choice and learn. Do not fill in the answers first. Do not memorize the questions and answers, but understand the answer and principles involved. On your test, the questions will likely be different from the samples. Questions are changed and new ones added. If you understand these past questions you should have success with any changes that arise. Tests may consist of several types of questions. We have additional books on each subject should more study be advisable or necessary for you. Finally, the more you study, the better prepared you will be. This book is intended to be the last thing you study before you walk into the examination room. Prior study of relevant texts is also recommended. NLC publishes some of these in our Fundamental Series. Knowledge and good sense are important factors in passing your exam. Good luck also helps. So now study this Passbook, absorb the material contained within and take that knowledge into the examination. Then do your best to pass that exam.

———

EXAMINATION SECTION

EXAMINATION SECTION
TEST 1

DIRECTIONS: Each question or incomplete statement is followed by several suggested
answers or completions. Select the one that BEST answers the question or
completes the statement. *PRINT THE LETTER OF THE CORRECT ANSWER
IN THE SPACE AT THE RIGHT.*

1. As a clerk in an office in a city agency, you have just been given a new assignment by   1.____
    your supervisor. The assignment was previously done by another clerk.
    Before beginning work on this assignment, it is MOST important that you

    A. find out who did the assignment previously
    B. understand your supervisor's instructions for doing the assignment
    C. notify the other clerks in the office that you have just received a new assignment
    D. understand how the assignment is related to the work of other clerks in the office

2. Assume that you are a clerk in a city department. Your supervisor has given you an   2.____
    important job that he wants completed as quickly as possible. You will be unable to com-
    plete the job by the end of the day, and you will be unable to work on the job in the next
    several days because you will be away from the office.
    Of the following, the MOST appropriate action for you to take before leaving the office
    at the end of the day is to

    A. lock your work in your desk so that the work will not be disturbed
    B. ask another clerk in the office to finish the job while you are away
    C. tell your supervisor how much of the job has been done and how much remains to
        be done
    D. leave a note on your supervisor's desk, advising him that you will continue to work
        on the job as soon as you return to the office

3. Assume that, as a newly appointed clerk in a city department, you are doing an assign-   3.____
    ment according to a method that your supervisor has told you to use. You believe that
    you would be less likely to make errors if you were to do the assignment by a different
    method, although the method your supervisor has told you to use is faster.
    For you to discuss your method with your supervisor would be

    A. *desirable* because he may not know the value of your method
    B. *undesirable* because he may know of your method and may prefer the faster one
    C. *desirable* because your method may show your supervisor that you are able to do
        accurate work
    D. *undesirable* because your method may not be as helpful to you as you believe it to
        be

4. Assume that you are responsible for receiving members of the public who visit your   4.____
    department for information. At a time when there are several persons seeking informa-
    tion, a man asks you for information in a rude and arrogant manner. Of the following, the
    BEST action for you to take in handling this man is to

    A. give him the information in the same manner in which he spoke to you
    B. ignore his request until he asks for the information in a more polite manner

C. give him the information politely, without commenting to him on his manner
D. ask him to request the information in a polite manner so as not to annoy other people seeking information

5. As a clerk in a city agency, you are assigned to issue publications to members of the public who request the applications in person. Your supervisor has told you that under no circumstances are you to issue more than one application to each person. A person enters the office and asks for two applications, explaining that he wants the second one for use in the event that he makes an error in filling out the application.
Of the following, the MOST appropriate action for you to take in this situation is to

    5.____

    A. give the person two applications since he may not know how to fill out the application
    B. ask your supervisor for permission to give the person two applications
    C. give one application to the person and advise him to come back later for another one
    D. issue one application to the person and inform him that only one application may be issued to an individual

6. Suppose that as a clerk in an office of a city department, you have been assigned by your supervisor to assist Mr. Jones, another clerk in the office, and to do his work in his absence. Part of Mr. Jones' duties are to give routine information to visitors who request the information. Several months later, shortly after Mr. Jones has begun a three-week vacation, a visitor enters the office and asks for some routine information which is available to the public. He explains that he previously had gotten similar information from Mr. Jones.
Of the following, the MOST advisable action for you to take is to

    6.____

    A. inform the visitor that Mr. Jones is on vacation but that you will attempt to obtain the information
    B. advise the visitor to return to the office when Mr. Jones will have returned from vacation
    C. tell the visitor that you will have Mr. Jones mail him the information as soon as he returns from vacation
    D. attempt to contact Mr. Jones to ask him whether the information should be given to the visitor

7. Miss Smith is a clerk in the information section of a city department.
Of the following, the MOST desirable way for Miss Smith to answer a telephone call to the section is to say,

    7.____

    A. "Hello. Miss Smith speaking."
    B. "Miss Smith speaking. May I ask who is calling?"
    C. "Hello. May I be of service to you?"
    D. "Information Section, Miss Smith."

8. When preparing papers for filing, it is NOT desirable to

    8.____

    A. smooth papers that are wrinkled
    B. use paper clips to keep related papers together in the files
    C. arrange the papers in the order in which they will be filed
    D. mend torn papers with cellophane tape

9. Assume that you are a clerk in the mail room of a city department. One of your duties is to open the letters addressed to the department and to route them to the appropriate offices. One of the letters you open evidently requires the attention of two different offices in the department.
In this situation, the one of the following which is the BEST action for you to take is to

    A. make two duplicate copies of the letter, send one to each office, and keep the original on file in the mail room
    B. send the letter to one of the offices with a request that the letter be forwarded to the second office
    C. return the letter to the writer with a request that he write separate letters to each of the two offices
    D. request the head of each office to send one of his employees to the mail room to decide what should be done with the letter

9.____

10. As a mail clerk in a city department, you are responsible for opening incoming mail and routing the letters to the appropriate offices in the department.
The one of the following situations in which it would be MOST appropriate for you to attach a letter to the envelope in which the letter arrives is when the

    A. name and address of the sender, which are on the envelope, are missing from the letter
    B. letter contains important or confidential information
    C. enclosures the envelope is supposed to contain are missing from the envelope
    D. envelope is not addressed to a specific office in the department

10.____

11. In writing a letter, it is important that the letter be paragraphed properly.
Of the following, the CHIEF value of proper paragraphing is to

    A. shorten the contents of the letter
    B. assist the writer by shortening the time required to write the letter
    C. aid the reader to understand the contents of the letter more readily
    D. reduce the time required to type the letter

11.____

12. A mailing list is a list containing the names and addresses of the individuals and organizations with which a public agency corresponds frequently. Such a list is sometimes kept on 3"x5" cards.
Of the following, the MOST important reason for an agency to keep its mailing list on cards is that

    A. the mailing list changes frequently
    B. more than one office in the agency uses the mailing list
    C. the mailing list is used frequently
    D. only part of the mailing list is used at any one time

12.____

13. Under a subject filing system, letters are filed in folders labeled according to subject matter. Assume that you have been asked to file a large number of letters under such a filing system.
Of the following, the FIRST step that you should take in filing these letters is to

    A. arrange the letters alphabetically under each subject
    B. determine under which subject each letter is to be filed

13.____

C. arrange the letters by date under each subject
D. prepare cross-references for each letter that should be filed under more than one subject

14. Your supervisor assigns you to file a number of letters in an alphabetical file drawer. In the course of your work, you notice that several letters in the file have been unintentionally misfiled.
Of the following, the MOST appropriate action for you to take in this situation is to   14._____

A. complete your filing assignment and then go through the file again to pick out any misfiled letters for refiling
B. leave the misfiled letters where they are in order to avoid disturbing the order of the file
C. put the misfiled letters in their proper places as you discover these letters
D. insert a note in the misfiled letters' proper places indicating where the misfiled letters may be found

15. Suppose that your supervisor gives you a folder containing a large number of letters arranged in the order of the dates they were received and a list of names of persons in alphabetical order. He asks you to determine, without disturbing the order of the letters, if there is a letter in the folder from each person on the list.
Of the following, the BEST method to use in doing this assignment is to   15._____

A. determine whether the number of letters in the folder is the same as the number of names on the list
B. look at each letter to see who wrote it, and then place a light check mark on each letter that has been written by a person on the list
C. prepare a list of the names of the writers of the letters that are in the folder, and then place a light check mark next to each of the names on this list if the name appears on the list of persons your supervisor gave you
D. look at each letter to see who wrote it, and then place a light check mark next to the name of the person on the list who wrote the letter

16. Whenever material is requested from a file under which the material is filed according to subject, the person requesting the material should be required to make out a requisition slip.
Of the following, the information that ordinarily would be LEAST useful to include on such a requisition slip is the   16._____

A. subject of the material requested
B. date the material is requested
C. reason why the material is being requested
D. name of the person requesting the material

17. A tickler file is GENERALLY used   17._____

A. as a reminder of work to be done
B. to store inactive records
C. as an index of the records contained in a filing system
D. to store miscellaneous important records

18. A listing adding machine prints, on a roll or strip of paper, the numbers added and their sum.   18._____
    Of the following, the CHIEF advantage of printing the numbers and their sum on the strip of paper is to

    A. provide a check on the accuracy of the machine
    B. show that the addition was done by machine
    C. permit the machine operator to make hand-written corrections in the numbers and their sum
    D. provide a record of the numbers and their sum

Questions 19-21.

DIRECTIONS: Questions 19 to 21 are to be answered SOLELY on the basis of the information contained in the following paragraph.

In order to organize records properly, it is necessary to start from their very beginning and to trace each copy of the record to find out how it is used, how long it is used, and what may finally be done with it. Although several copies of the record are made, one copy should be marked as the copy of record. This is the formal legal copy, held to meet the requirements of the law. The other copies may be retained for brief periods for reference purposes, but these copies should not be kept after their usefulness as reference ends. There is another reason for tracing records through the office and that is to determine how long it takes the copy of record to reach the central file. The copy of record must not be kept longer than necessary by the section of the office which has prepared it, but should be sent to the central file as soon as possible so that it can be available to the various sections of the office. The central file can make the copy of record available to the various sections of the office at an early date only if it arrives at the central file as quickly as possible. Just as soon as its immediate or active service period is ended, the copy of record should be removed from the central file and put into the inactive file in the office to be stored for whatever length of time may be necessary to meet legal requirements, and then destroyed.

19. According to the above paragraph, a reason for tracing records through an office is to   19._____

    A. determine how long the central file must keep the records
    B. organize records properly
    C. find out how many copies of each record are required
    D. identify the copy of record

20. According to the above paragraph, in order for the central file to have the copy of record available as soon as possible for the various sections of the office, it is MOST important that the   20._____

    A. copy of record to be sent to the central file meets the requirements of the law
    B. copy of record is not kept in the inactive file too long
    C. section preparing the copy of record does not unduly delay in sending it to the central file
    D. central file does not keep the copy of record beyond its active service period

21. According to the above paragraph, the length of time a copy of a record is kept in the inactive file of an office depends CHIEFLY on the 21.____

    A. requirements of the law
    B. length of time that is required to trace the copy of record through the office
    C. use that is made of the copy of record
    D. length of the period that the copy of record is used for reference purposes

22. As a clerk, you may be assigned the duty of opening and sorting the mail coming to your department. 22.____
    The one of the following which is the BEST reason for not discarding the envelopes in which letters come from members of the public until you have glanced at the letters is that

    A. it is rarely necessary to return a letter to the writer in the original envelope
    B. the subject of a letter can, of course, be determined only from the letter itself
    C. the envelopes should usually be filed together with the letters
    D. members of the public frequently neglect to include a return address in their letters

23. Suppose that your supervisor has asked you and another clerk to proofread a letter. The other clerk is reading rapidly to you from the original copy while you are checking the letter. 23.____
    For you to interrupt his reading and make an immediate notation of each error you find is

    A. *wise;* you might otherwise overlook an error
    B. *foolish;* such action slows down the reading
    C. *foolish;* such action demonstrates that the copy is not accurate
    D. *wise;* such action demonstrates that the rate of reading may be increased

24. Suppose that the name files in your office contain filing guides on which appear the letters of the alphabet. The letters X, Y, and Z, unlike the other letters of the alphabet, are grouped together and appear on a single guide. 24.____
    Of the following, the BEST reason for combining these three letters into a single filing unit is probably that

    A. provision must be made for expanding the file if that should become necessary
    B. there is usually insufficient room for filing guides towards the end of a long file
    C. the letters X, Y, and Z are at the end of the alphabet
    D. relatively few names begin with these letters of the alphabet

25. You are requested by your supervisor to replace each card you take out of the files with an *out-of-file* slip. The *out-of-file* slip indicates which card has been removed from the file and where the card may be found. Of the following, the CHIEF value of the *out-of-file* slip is that a clerk looking for a card which happens to have been removed by another clerk 25.____

    A. will know that the card has been returned to the file
    B. can substitute the *out-of-file* slip for the original card
    C. will not waste time searching for the card under the impression that it has been misfiled
    D. is not likely to misfile a card he has been using for some other purpose

26. The sum of 284.5, 3016.24, 8.9736, and 94.15 is MOST NEARLY   26._____

    A. 3402.9   B. 3403.0   C. 3403.9   D. 4036.1

27. If 8394.6 is divided by 29.17, the result is MOST NEARLY   27._____

    A. 288   B. 347   C. 2880   D. 3470

28. If two numbers are multiplied together, the result is 3752. If one of the two numbers is 56,   28._____
the other number is

    A. 41   B. 15   C. 109   D. 67

29. The sum of the fractions 1/4, 2/3, 3/8, 5/6, and 3/4 is   29._____

    A. 20/33   B. 1 19/24   C. 2 1/4   D. 2 7/8

30. The fraction 7/16 expressed as a decimal is   30._____

    A. .1120   B. .2286   C. .4375   D. .4850

31. If .10 is divided by 50, the result is   31._____

    A. .002   B. .02   C. .2   D. 2

32. The number 60 is 40% of   32._____

    A. 24   B. 84   C. 96   D. 150

33. If 3/8 of a number is 96, the number is   33._____

    A. 132   B. 36   C. 256   D. 156

34. A city department uses an average of 25 10-cent, 35 15-cent, and 350 20-cent postage   34._____
stamps each day. The total cost of stamps used by the department in a five-day period is

    A. $14.75   B. $77.75   C. $145.25   D. $388.75

35. A city department issued 12,000 applications in 2007. The number of applications that   35._____
the department issued in 2005 was 25% greater than the number it issued in 2007.
If the department issued 10% fewer applications in 2003 than it did in 2005, the number it issued in 2003 was

    A. 16,500   B. 13,500   C. 9,900   D. 8,100

36. A clerk can add 40 columns of figures an hour by using an adding machine and 20 col-   36._____
umns of figures an hour without using an adding machine.
The total number of hours it would take him to add 200 columns if he does 3/5 of the
work by machine and the rest without the machine is

    A. 6   B. 7   C. 8   D. 9

37. In 2004, a city department bought 500 dozen pencils at 40 cents per dozen. In 2007, only   37._____
75% as many pencils were bought as were bought in 2004, but the price was 20% higher
than the 2004 price.
The total cost of the pencils bought in 2007 was

    A. $180   B. $187.50   C. $240   D. $250

38. A clerk is assigned to check the accuracy of the entries on 490 forms. He checks 40 forms an hour. After working one hour on this task, he is joined by another clerk, who checks these forms at the rate of 35 an hour.
The total number of hours required to do the entire assignment is

    A. 5   B. 6   C. 7   D. 8

38.____

39. Assume that there are a total of 420 employees in a city agency. Thirty percent of the employees are clerks, and 1/7 are typists.
The difference between the number of clerks and the number of typists is

    A. 126   B. 66   C. 186   D. 80

39.____

40. Assume that a duplicating machine produces copies of a bulletin at a cost of 2 cents per copy. The machine produces 120 copies of the bulletin per minute.
If the cost of producing a certain number of copies was $12, how many minutes of operation did it take the machine to produce this number of copies?

    A. 5   B. 2   C. 10   D. 6

40.____

Questions 41-63.

DIRECTIONS: Each of Questions 41 to 63 consists of a word in capitals followed by four suggested meanings of the word. For each question, indicate in the correspondingly numbered space at the right the letter preceding the word which means MOST NEARLY the same as the word in capitals.

41. ADAPT

    A. make suitable   B. advise
    C. do away with   D. propose

41.____

42. CAPACITY

    A. need   B. willingness
    C. ability   D. curiosity

42.____

43. EXEMPT

    A. defend   B. excuse   C. refuse   D. expect

43.____

44. CONFORM

    A. conceal from view   B. remember
    C. be in agreement   D. complain

44.____

45. DILEMMA

    A. decision   B. mistake   C. violence   D. predicament

45.____

46. OPPORTUNE

    A. temporary   B. timely   C. sudden   D. recent

46.____

47. DEVIATE

    A. turn aside   B. deny
    C. come to a halt   D. disturb

47.____

48. COMPILE   48.____

    A. confuse   B. support   C. compare   D. gather

49. MANIPULATE   49.____

    A. attempt   B. add incorrectly
    C. handle   D. investigate closely

50. POTENTIAL   50.____

    A. useful   B. possible   C. welcome   D. rare

KEY (CORRECT ANSWER)

1. B	11. C	21. A	31. A	41. A
2. C	12. A	22. D	32. D	42. C
3. A	13. B	23. A	33. C	43. B
4. C	14. C	24. D	34. D	44. C
5. D	15. D	25. C	35. B	45. D
6. A	16. C	26. C	36. B	46. B
7. D	17. A	27. A	37. A	47. A
8. B	18. D	28. D	38. C	48. D
9. B	19. B	29. D	39. B	49. C
10. A	20. C	30. C	40. A	50. B

TEST 2

DIRECTIONS: Each question or incomplete statement is followed by several suggested answers or completions. Select the one that BEST answers the question or completes the statement. *PRINT THE LETTER OF THE CORRECT ANSWER IN THE SPACE AT THE RIGHT.*

1. AUTHORIZE 1.____

    A. write   B. permit   C. request   D. recommend

2. ASSESS 2.____

    A. set a value on   B. belong
    C. think highly of   D. increase

3. CONVENTIONAL 3.____

    A. democratic   B. convenient   C. modern   D. customary

4. DEPLETE 4.____

    A. replace   B. exhaust   C. review   D. withhold

5. INTERVENE 5.____

    A. sympathize with   B. differ
    C. ask for an opinion   D. interfere

6. HAZARDOUS 6.____

    A. dangerous   B. unusual   C. slow   D. difficult

7. SUBSTANTIATE 7.____

    A. replace   B. suggest   C. verify   D. suffer

8. DISCORD 8.____

    A. remainder   B. disagreement   C. pressure   D. dishonest

9. TENACIOUS 9.____

    A. vicious   B. irritable   C. truthful   D. unyielding

10. ALLEVIATE 10.____

    A. relieve   B. appreciate   C. succeed   D. admit

11. FALLACY 11.____

    A. basis   B. false idea
    C. guilt   D. lack of respect

12. SCRUTINIZE 12.____

    A. reject   B. bring about
    C. examine   D. insist upon

13. IMMINENT 13.____

    A. anxious   B. well-known
    C. important   D. about to happen

Questions 14-25.

DIRECTIONS: Each of Questions 14 to 25 consists of a sentence which may be classified appropriately under one of the following four categories:
    A. incorrect because of faulty grammar or sentence structure
    B. incorrect because of faulty punctuation
    C. incorrect because of faulty capitalization
    D. correct

        Examine each sentence carefully. Then, in the correspondingly numbered space at the right, indicate the letter preceding the category which is the BEST of the four suggested above. Each incorrect sentence contains only one type of error. Consider a sentence correct if it contains no errors, although there may be other correct ways of expressing the same thought.

14. All the clerks, including those who have been appointed recently are required to work on the new assignment.   14._____

15. The office manager asked each employee to work one Saturday a month.   15._____

16. Neither Mr. Smith nor Mr. Jones was able to finish his assignment on time.   16._____

17. The task of filing these cards is to be divided equally between you and he.   17._____

18. He is an employee whom we consider to be efficient.   18._____

19. I believe that the new employees are not as punctual as us.   19._____

20. The employees, working in this office, are to be congratulated for their work.   20._____

21. The supervisor entered the room and said, "The work must be completed today."   21._____

22. The employees were given their assignments and, they were asked to begin work immediately.   22._____

23. The letter will be sent to the United States senate this week.   23._____

24. When the supervisor entered the room, he noticed that the book was laying on the desk.   24._____

25. The price of the pens were higher than the price of the pencils.   25._____

Questions 26-35.

DIRECTIONS: Each of Questions 26 to 35 consists of a group of four words. One word in each group is INCORRECTLY spelled. For each question, indicate in the correspondingly numbered space at the right, the letter preceding the word which is INCORRECTLY spelled.

26.	A. grateful	B. fundimental	C. census	D. analysis	26.____
27.	A. installment	B. retrieve	C. concede	D. dissapear	27.____
28.	A. accidentaly	B. dismissal	C. conscientious	D. indelible	28.____
29.	A. perceive	B. carreer	C. anticipate	D. acquire	29.____
30.	A. facillity	B. reimburse	C. assortment	D. guidance	30.____
31.	A. plentiful	B. across	C. advantagous	D. similar	31.____
32.	A. omission	B. pamphlet	C. guarrantee	D. repel	32.____
33.	A. maintenance	B. always	C. liable	D. anouncement	33.____
34.	A. exaggerate	B. sieze	C. condemn	D. commit	34.____
35.	A. pospone	B. altogether	C. grievance	D. excessive	35.____

Questions 36-41.

DIRECTIONS: Questions 36 to 41 are to be answered SOLELY on the basis of the information and directions given below.

Assume that you are a clerk assigned to the personnel bureau of a department. Your supervisor has asked you to classify the employees in your agency into the following four groups:

A. Female employees who are college graduates, who are less than 35 years of age, and who earn at least $36,000 a year;
B. Male employees who are not college graduates, who are less than 35 years of age, and who earn at least $38,000 a year but not more than $44,000 a year;
C. Female employees who are 35 years of age or older, who are not college graduates, and who earn at least $30,000 a year but less than $36,000 a year;
D. Male employees who are college graduates, who are 35 years of age or older, and who earn more than $44,000 a year.

NOTE: In each question, consider only the information which will assist you in classifying each employee. Any information which is of no assistance in classifying an employee should not be considered.

SAMPLE: Mr. Smith, a city resident, is 60 years of age, and is a college graduate. His salary is $45,600 a year.

The correct answer to this sample is D, since the employee is a male college graduate, is more than 35 years of age, and earns more than $44,000 a year.
Questions 36 to 41 contain information from the personnel records in the department. For each question, indicate in the correspondingly numbered space at the right the letter preceding the appropriate group into which you would place each employee.

36. Mrs. Brown is a 33-year-old accountant who was graduated from college with honors. Her present annual salary is $43,480.   36.____

37. Mr. Queen has had two promotions since beginning work for the department eight years ago at the age of 29. A college graduate, he receives $50,800 a year as supervisor in charge of a bureau. 37._____

38. Miss Arthur earns $35,400 a year and has worked in the department for five years. Now 36 years of age, she attends high school in the evenings and hopes to obtain a high school diploma. 38._____

39. At 34 years of age, Mr. Smith earns $43,960 per annum. After he was graduated from high school, he attended college for two years, but he did not complete his college course. 39._____

40. Mr. Rose is a 28-year-old high school graduate earning $38,200 a year. He intends to attend college in the evenings to study public administration. 40._____

41. Mr. Johnson, a veteran, attended college in the evenings for six years before he obtained a degree in engineering. At 37 years of age, he earns an annual salary of $53,200. 41._____

Questions 42-50.

DIRECTIONS: Each of Questions 42 to 50 consists of four names. For each question, select the one of the four names that should be THIRD if the four names were arranged in alphabetical order in accordance with the Rules of Alphabetical Filing given below. Read these rules carefully. Then, for each question indicate in the correspondingly numbered space at the right the letter preceding the name that should be THIRD in alphabetical order.

RULES FOR ALPHABETICAL FILING

NAMES OF INDIVIDUALS

(1) The names of individuals are filed in strict alphabetical order: first according to the last name, then according to first name or initial, and finally according to middle name or initial. For example: William Jones precedes George Kirk, and Arthur S. Blake precedes Charles M. Blake.

(2) When the last names are identical, the one with an initial instead of a first name precedes the one with a first name beginning with the same initial. For example: J. Green precedes Joseph Green.

(3) When identical last names also have identical first names, the one without a middle name or initial precedes the one with a middle name or initial. For example: Robert Jackson precedes both Robert C. Jackson and Robert Chester Jackson.

(4) When last names are identical and the first names are also identical, the one with a middle initial precedes the one with a middle name beginning with the same initial. For example: Peter A. Brown precedes Peter Alvin Brown.

(5) Prefixes such as De, El, La, and Van are considered parts of the names they precede. For example: Wilfred De Wald precedes Alexander Duval.

(6) Last names beginning with "Mac" or "Mc" are filed as spelled.

(7)   *Abbreviated names are treated as if they were spelled out. For example: Jos. is filed as Joseph, and Robt. is filed as Robert.*

(8)   *Titles and designations such as Dr., Mrs., Prof. are disregarded in filing.*

NAMES OF BUSINESS ORGANIZATIONS

(1)   *The names of business organisations are filed exactly as written, except that an organization bearing the name of an individual is filed alphabetically according to the name of the individual in accordance with the rules for filing names of individuals given above. For example: Thomas Allison Machine Company precedes Northern Baking Company.*

(2)   *When numerals occur in a name, they are treated as if they were spelled out. For example: 6 stands for six, and 4th stands for fourth.*

(3)   *When the following words occur in names, they are disregarded: the, of, and.*

SAMPLE:

    A.   Fred Town   (2)
    B.   Jack Towne   (3)
    C.   D. Town   (1)
    D.   Jack S. Towne (4)

The numbers in parentheses indicate the proper alphabetical order in which these names should be filed. Since the name that should be filed THIRD is Jack Towne, the answer is B.

42.   A.   Herbert Restman   42._____
        B.   H. Restman
        C.   Harry Restmore
        D.   H. Restmore

43.   A.   Martha Eastwood   43._____
        B.   Martha E. Eastwood
        C.   Martha Edna Eastwood
        D.   M. Eastwood

44.   A.   Timothy Macalan   44._____
        B.   Fred McAlden
        C.   Thomas MacAllister
        D.   Mrs. Frank McAllen

45.   A.   Elm Trading Co.   45._____
        B.   El Dorado Trucking Corp.
        C.   James Eldred Jewelry Store
        D.   Eldridge Printing, Inc.

46.   A.   Edward La Gabriel   46._____
        B.   Marie Doris Gabriel
        C.   Marjorie N. Gabriel
        D.   Marjorie N. Gabriel

47. A. Peter La Vance 47.____
     B. George Van Meer
     C. Wallace De Vance
     D. Leonard Vance

48. A. Fifth Avenue Book Shop 48.____
     B. Mr. Wm. A. Fifner
     C. 52nd Street Association
     D. Robert B. Fiffner

49. A. Dr. Chas. D. Peterson 49.____
     B. Miss Irene F. Petersen
     C. Lawrence E. Peterson
     D. Prof. N.A. Petersen

50. A. 71st Street Theater 50.____
     B. The Seven Seas Corp.
     C. 7th Ave. Service Co.
     D. Walter R. Sevan and Co.

KEY (CORRECT ANSWERS)

1.	B	11.	B	21.	D	31.	C	41.	D
2.	A	12.	C	22.	B	32.	C	42.	D
3.	D	13.	D	23.	C	33.	D	43.	B
4.	B	14.	B	24.	A	34.	B	44.	B
5.	D	15.	C	25.	A	35.	A	45.	D
6.	A	16.	D	26.	B	36.	A	46.	C
7.	C	17.	A	27.	D	37.	D	47.	D
8.	B	18.	D	28.	A	38.	C	48.	A
9.	D	19.	A	29.	B	39.	B	49.	A
10.	A	20.	B	30.	A	40.	B	50.	C

EXAMINATION SECTION
TEST 1

DIRECTIONS: Each question or incomplete statement is followed by several suggested answers or completions. Select the one that BEST answers the question or completes the statement. *PRINT THE LETTER OF THE CORRECT ANSWER IN THE SPACE AT THE RIGHT.*

1. Assume that you are appointed as a clerk in a city department. As a new employee, you are PRIMARILY expected to

    A. inform your supervisor of the amount of training you will need to handle your new job
    B. perform your work in accordance with the instructions given you by your supervisor
    C. show your supervisor that you like the work you are assigned to do
    D. prove to your supervisor that you are able to handle your new job with very little instruction

1._____

2. Assume that you are a clerk in a city agency. One day, your supervisor tells you that he will be too busy to speak to visitors coming to the office that day. He instructs you to refer all visitors, including those with urgent business, to Mr. Brown, one of his assistants. During the day, a visitor enters the office and tells you that he wishes to speak to your supervisor on an important matter. Of the following, the MOST appropriate course of action for you to take in this situation is to

    A. advise the visitor that Mr. Brown may be better informed than your supervisor on the matter
    B. notify your supervisor that a visitor wishes to speak to him on an important matter
    C. ask the visitor to return at another time when your supervisor will be able to speak to him
    D. inform the visitor that your supervisor is not available but that Mr. Brown will attempt to help him

2._____

3. As a clerk in the mail room of a large city department, you are responsible for opening incoming letters and for routing them to the appropriate offices in the department. The MOST important reason why you should know thoroughly the functions of the various offices in the department is that

    A. letters are sometimes addressed only to the department rather than to a specific office in the department
    B. each office may have its own method of answering letters
    C. a letter addressed only to the department would not have to be opened before forwarding it to the proper office
    D. an accurate listing of the locations of offices and employees in the department is essential to a mail room clerk

3._____

4. Suppose that one of your duties as a clerk in a city department is to answer letters requesting information. One such letter requests some information that you can supply immediately and other information which you know will not be available for several weeks. It is evident that the writer of the letter is not aware that some of the information is not available immediately.
Of the following, the MOST appropriate action for you to take in this matter is to

4._____

A. supply the writer with the information that is available immediately and ask him to write for the rest of the information at a later date
B. supply the writer with the information that is available immediately and inform him that the rest of the information will be sent in several weeks
C. write to the person requesting the information, asking him to make his request again in several weeks when all the information will be available
D. wait until the rest of the information becomes available in several weeks and then send all the information at once

5. Assume that you have been given an unalphabetized list of 1,000 employees in your agency and a set of unalphabetized payroll cards. You have been asked to determine if, for each name on the list, there is a corresponding payroll card.
Of the following, the BEST reason for first alphabetizing the payroll cards is that

A. each name on the list could then be more easily checked against the payroll cards
B. it then becomes easier to alphabetize the names on the list
C. introducing an additional step in the checking process produces a more compli-cated procedure
D. you may obtain additional information from the payroll cards to help you check the names

6. Suppose that you have just been appointed as a clerk in a city department. Although your supervisor has given you instructions for filing personnel cards, you still do not fully understand how to file them.
For you to ask your supervisor to explain more fully how you are to file the cards would be desirable CHIEFLY because

A. you will prove to your supervisor that you intend to do a good job
B. your supervisor will be willing to explain the instructions more fully
C. you will be better prepared to do the assignment if you fully understand what you are to do
D. new employees cannot be expected to do their work properly without having instructions repeated

7. In many cases, it becomes evident that a filing problem exists only after a paper has been filed and cannot be found.
On the basis of the above statement, it is MOST accurate to state that

A. filing problems become evident before errors in filing have been discovered
B. a filing problem is solved when a misfiled paper is found
C. even a careful file clerk may create a filing problem
D. a filing problem may not become apparent until a filed paper cannot be located

8. Assume that you are a newly appointed clerk in a large office of a city department. You believe that the method used for doing a certain type of work in the office should be changed.
Of the following, the MOST important reason why you should suggest the change to your supervisor is that

A. supervisors are usually reluctant to make changes unless they are necessary
B. you are expected, as a new employee, to suggest important improvements in office work

C.   your suggestion may improve the method used for this type of work
D.   it is more important to make changes in large offices than in small ones

9.   The average citizen is not interested in the amount of work assigned to public employees   9._____
or the pressure under which they sometimes work. If a public employee fails to give
prompt and courteous service, the average citizen estimates the efficiency of all public
employees accordingly.
On the basis of the above passage, the MOST accurate of the following statements is
that

    A.   the average citizen usually realizes that the efficiency of public employees depends
         upon the amount of work assigned to them
    B.   the average citizen's attitude toward all public employees may be influenced by the
         service rendered by an individual public employee
    C.   the pressure of work duties often causes public employees to render unsatisfactory
         service to the public
    D.   the average citizen may help to improve the efficiency of public employees by tak-
         ing an interest in their work

10.   Suppose that you have been asked to proofread a copy of a report with another clerk.   10._____
The other clerk is to read to you from the original report while you check the copy for
errors.
For you to make a notation of each error as you detect it rather than wait until the end
of the proofreading to note all the errors at once would be

    A.   *desirable;* you would be less likely to overlook noting an error
    B.   *undesirable;* the original report may not be correct
    C.   *desirable;* the more clearly the other clerk reads, the more accurately you will be
         able to detect and note errors
    D.   *undesirable;* the notations made during the proofreading may not be legible later

11.   If the methods used in an office seem to be faulty, an employee should offer constructive   11._____
suggestions instead of mere criticisms of the methods.
On the basis of this statement, it is MOST accurate to state that

    A.   the methods used in an office should be criticized only if they cannot be improved
    B.   most of the problems arising in an office can be overcome satisfactorily by
         employee suggestions
    C.   an employee should suggest improvements for existing poor methods rather than
         only find fault with them
    D.   the quality of suggestions submitted by employees depends upon the methods
         used in an office

12.   The abbreviation *e.g.* ORDINARILY means   12._____

    A.   instead of   B.   express charges guaranteed
    C.   for example   D.   excellent grade

13.   As a clerk assigned to keeping payroll records in your department, you are instructed by   13._____
your supervisor to use a new method for keeping the records. You think that the new
method will be less effective than the one you are now using.
In this situation, it would be MOST advisable for you to

A. use the new method to keep the records even if you think it may be less effective
B. continue to use the method you consider to be more effective without saying any-thing to your supervisor
C. use the method you consider to be more effective and then tell your supervisor your reasons for doing so
D. use the new method only if you can improve its effectiveness

14. The term that describes the programs installed on an office computer is   14._____

    A. interface   B. hardware
    C. network   D. software

15. An examination of the financial records of a business firm or public agency in order to   15._____
    determine its true financial condition is called a(n)

    A. budget   B. voucher
    C. audit   D. appropriation

Questions 16-17.

DIRECTIONS: Questions 16 and 17 are to be answered SOLELY on the basis of the informa-tion contained in the following statement.

   A duplex envelope is an envelope composed of two sections securely fastened together so that they become one mailing piece. This type of envelope makes it possible for a first class letter to be delivered simultaneously with third or fourth class matter and yet not require payment of the much higher first class postage rate on the entire mailing. First class postage is paid only on the letter which goes in the small compartment, third or fourth class postage being paid on the contents of the larger compartment. The larger compartment generally has an ungummed flap or clasp for sealing. The first class or smaller compartment has a gummed flap for sealing. Postal regulations require that the exact amount of postage applicable to each compartment be separately attached to it.

16. On the basis of this paragraph, it is MOST accurate to state that   16._____

    A. the smaller compartment is placed inside the larger compartment before mailing
    B. the two compartments may be detached and mailed separately
    C. two classes of mailing matter may be mailed as a unit at two different postage rates
    D. the more expensive postage rate is paid on the matter in the larger compartment

17. When a duplex envelope is used, the   17._____

    A. first class compartment may be sealed with a clasp
    B. correct amount of postage must be placed on each compartment
    C. compartment containing third or fourth class mail requires a gummed flap for seal-ing
    D. full amount of postage for both compartments may be placed on the larger com-partment

18. The MOST accurate of the following statements is that a City Charter   18._____

    A. lists the names, titles, and salaries of the heads of the various city agencies
    B. shows the funds allocated to each city agency

C. contains all the local laws passed by the City Council
D. describes the functions of city agencies

19. A period of inflation may generally BEST be described as a period in which the   19._____

A. hourly and weekly wages paid to employees decline rapidly
B. purchasing power of pensions and other fixed incomes increases
C. purchasing power of money declines
D. number of unemployed persons increases sharply

20. You have been asked by your supervisor to code about 500 cards on each of six different   20._____
classification bases according to a previously prepared key. Halfway through the task,
you realize suddenly that on the last few cards, you have begun to use incorrect code
numbers in coding one particular classification. You know that your work will be checked
by another clerk.
For you to go back to the beginning of the cards immediately and to check the coding
of only the particular classification in the coding of which you have erred would be
commendable CHIEFLY because

A. all the cards will be checked carefully by another clerk
B. you have probably misinterpreted the entire coding key
C. there is an especially strong likelihood of error in the coding of the particular classi-
fication
D. you have almost completed the task and no time will be wasted

21. Suppose that it is the practice in your department to file all the correspondence with one   21._____
individual in a single folder and to file the most recent letters first in the folder.
Of the following, the BEST justification for placing the most recent letter first rather than
last in the folder is that, in general,

A. letters placed in front of a folder are usually less accessible
B. requests for previous correspondence from the files usually concern letters filed
relatively recently
C. letters in a folder can usually be located most quickly when they are filed in a definite order
D. filing can usually be accomplished very quickly when letters are placed in a folder
without reference to date

22. While filing cards in an alphabetical file, you notice a card which is not in its correct   22._____
alphabetical order.
Of the following, the BEST action for you to take is to

A. show the card to your supervisor and ask him whether that card has been reported
lost
B. leave the card where it is, but inform the other clerks who use the file exactly where
they may find the card if they need it
C. file a cross-reference card in the place where the card should have been filed
D. make a written notation of where you can find the card in the event that your supervisor asks you for it

23. The sum of 637.894, 8352.16, 4.8673, and 301.5 is MOST NEARLY   23._____

A. 8989.5   B. 9021.35   C. 9294.9   D. 9296.4

24. If 30 is divided by .06, the result is   24._____

    A. 5   B. 5   C. 500   D. 5000

25. The sum of the fractions 1/3, 4/6, 1/2, 3/4 and 1/12 is   25._____

    A. 3 1/4   B. 2 1/3   C. 2 1/6   D. 1 11/12

26. If 96934.42 is divided by 53.496, the result is MOST NEARLY   26._____

    A. 181   B. 552   C. 1810   D. 5520

27. If 25% of a number is 48, the number is   27._____

    A. 12   B. 60   C. 144   D. 192

28. The average number of reports filed per day by a clerk during a five-day week was 720. 28._____
He filed 610 reports the first day, 720 reports the second day, 740 reports the third day, and 755 reports the fourth day.
The number of reports he filed the fifth day was

    A. 748   B. 165   C. 775   D. 565

29. The number 88 is 2/5 of   29._____

    A. 123   B. 141   C. 220   D. 440

30. If the product of 8.3 multiplied by .42 is subtracted from the product of 156 multiplied by 30._____
.09, the result is MOST NEARLY

    A. 10.6   B. 13.7   C. 17.5   D. 20.8

31. A city department employs 1400 people, of whom 35% are clerks and 1/8 are stenogra-   31._____
phers.
The number of employees in the department who are neither clerks nor stenographers
is

    A. 640   B. 665   C. 735   D. 760

32. Assume that there are 190 papers to be filed and that Clerk A and Clerk B are assigned 32._____
to file these papers. If Clerk A files 40 papers more than Clerk B, then the number of
papers that Clerk A files is

    A. 75   B. 110   C. 115   D. 150

33. A stock clerk had on hand the following items: 33._____
   500   pads, each worth four cents
   130   pencils, each worth three cents
    50   dozen rubber bands, worth two cents a dozen
If, from this stock, he issued 125 pads, 45 pencils, and 48 rubber bands, the value of
the remaining stock would be

    A. $6.43   B. $8.95   C. $17.63   D. $18.47

34. An assignment is completed by 32 clerks in 22 days. Assuming that all the clerks work at 34._____
the same rate of speed, the number of clerks that would be needed to complete this
assignment in 16 days is

A. 27   B. 38   C. 44   D. 52

35. A department head hired a total of 60 temporary employees to handle a seasonal increase in the department's workload. The following lists the number of temporary employees hired, their rates of pay, and the duration of their employment:
One-third of the total were hired as clerks, each at the rate of $13,750 a year, for two months
30 percent of the total were hired as office machine operators, each at the rate of $15,750 a year, for four months
22 stenographers were hired, each at the rate of $15,000 a year, for three months
The total amount paid to these temporary employees was MOST NEARLY

    A. $890,000   B. $225,000   C. $325,000   D. $196,000

35.____

36. Assume that there are 2300 employees in a city agency. Also assume that five percent of these employees are accountants, that 80 percent of the accountants have college degrees, and that one-half of the accountants who have college degrees have five years of experience.
Then the number of employees in the agency who are accountants with college degrees and five years of experience is

    A. 46   B. 51   C. 460   D. 920

36.____

Questions 37-50.

DIRECTIONS: Each of Questions 37 to 50 consists of a word in capitals followed by four suggested meanings of the word. For each question, indicate in the correspondingly numbered space at the right the letter preceding the word which means MOST NEARLY the same as the word in capitals.

37. AUXILIARY   37.____

    A. unofficial   B. available   C. temporary   D. aiding

38. DELETE   38.____

    A. explain   B. delay   C. erase   D. conceal

39. REFUTE   39.____

    A. receive   B. endorse   C. disprove   D. decline

40. CANDID   40.____

    A. correct   B. hasty   C. careful   D. frank

41. INFRACTION   41.____

    A. violation   B. investigation   C. punishment   D. part

42. OBJECTIVE   42.____

    A. method   B. goal   C. importance   D. fault

43. CONCUR   43.____

    A. agree   B. demand   C. control   D. create

44. JUSTIFY   44._____

    A. defend   B. understand   C. complete   D. request

45. INFER   45._____

    A. impress   B. conclude   C. intrude   D. decrease

46. CONSTRUE   46._____

    A. suggest   B. predict   C. interpret   D. urge

47. TRIVIAL   47._____

    A. unexpected   B. exact   C. unnecessary   D. petty

48. OPTIONAL   48._____

    A. useful   B. voluntary   C. valuable   D. obvious

49. SUBSEQUENT   49._____

    A. following   B. successful   C. permanent   D. simple

50. REVISE   50._____

    A. introduce   B. explain   C. begin   D. change

KEY (CORRECT ANSWERS)

1. B	11. C	21. B	31. C	41. A
2. D	12. C	22. A	32. C	42. B
3. A	13. A	23. D	33. D	43. A
4. B	14. D	24. C	34. C	44. A
5. A	15. C	25. B	35. B	45. B
6. C	16. C	26. C	36. A	46. C
7. D	17. B	27. D	37. D	47. D
8. C	18. D	28. C	38. C	48. B
9. B	19. C	29. C	39. C	49. A
10. A	20. C	30. A	40. D	50. D

TEST 2

DIRECTIONS: Each of Questions 1 to 9 consists of a word in capitals followed by four suggested meanings of the word. For each question, indicate in the correspondingly numbered space at the right the letter preceding the word which means
MOST NEARLY the same as the word in capitals.

1. CONCISE   1._____

  A. hidden   B. complicated   C. compact   D. recent

2. PROSPECTIVE   2._____

  A. anticipated   B. patient   C. influential   D. shrewd

3. STIMULATE   3._____

  A. regulate   B. arouse   C. imitate   D. strengthen

4. EXPEDITE   4._____

  A. exceed   B. expand   C. solve   D. hasten

5. RENOUNCE   5._____

  A. remind   B. raise   C. reject   D. restore

6. SURMISE   6._____

  A. inform   B. suppose   C. convince   D. pretend

7. FLUCTUATE   7._____

  A. vary   B. divide   C. improve   D. irritate

8. PERTINENT   8._____

  A. attractive   B. related   C. practical   D. lasting

9. CENSURE   9._____

  A. confess   B. count   C. confirm   D. criticize

Questions 10-14.

DIRECTIONS: Each of Questions 10 to 14 consists of a sentence which may be classified
appropriately under one of the following four categories:
   A. incorrect because of faulty grammar or sentence structure
   B. incorrect because of faulty punctuation
   C. incorrect because of faulty capitalization
   D. correct

Examine each sentence carefully. Then, in the correspondingly numbered
space at the right, indicate the letter preceding the category which is the BEST
of the four suggested above. Each incorrect sentence contains only one type
of error. Consider a sentence correct if it contains none of the types of errors
mentioned, although there may be other correct ways of expressing the same
thought.

10. We have learned that there was more than twelve people present at the meeting.   10.____

11. Every one of the employees is able to do this kind of work.   11.____

12. Neither the supervisor nor his assistant are in the office today.   12.____

13. The office manager announced that any clerk, who volunteered for the assignment,   13.____
    would be rewarded.

14. After looking carefully in all the files, the letter was finally found on a desk.   14.____

15. In answer to the clerk's question, the supervisor said, "this assignment must be com-   15.____
    pleted today."

16. The office manager says that he can permit only you and me to go to the meeting.   16.____

17. The supervisor refused to state who he would assign to the reception unit.   17.____

18. At the last meeting, he said that he would interview us in September.   18.____

19. Mr. Jones, who is one of our most experienced employees has been placed in charge of   19.____
    the main office.

20. I think that this adding machine is the most useful of the two we have in our office.   20.____

21. Between you and I, our new stenographer is not as competent as our former stenogra-   21.____
    pher.

22. The new assignment should be given to whoever can do the work rapidly.   22.____

23. Mrs. Smith, as well as three other typists, was assigned to the new office.   23.____

24. The staff assembled for the conference on time but, the main speaker arrived late.   24.____

Questions 25-34.

DIRECTIONS: Each of Questions 25 to 34 consists of a group of four words. One word in
each group is INCORRECTLY spelled. For each question, indicate in the correspondingly numbered space at the right the letter preceding the word which
is INCORRECTLY spelled.

25.	A. arguing	B. correspon-dance	C. forfeit	D. dissension	25.____
26.	A. occasion	B. description	C. prejudice	D. elegible	26.____
27.	A. accomodate	B. initiative	C. changeable	D. enroll	27.____
28.	A. temporary	B. insistent	C. benificial	D. separate	28.____
29.	A. achieve	B. dissappoint	C. unanimous	D. judgment	29.____

30.	A.	procede	B.	publicly	C.	sincerity	D.	successful	30.____
31.	A.	deceive	B.	goverment	C.	preferable	D.	repetitive	31.____
32.	A.	emphasis	B.	skillful	C.	advisible	D.	optimistic	32.____
33.	A.	tendency	B.	rescind	C.	crucial	D.	noticable	33.____
34.	A.	privelege	B.	abbreviate	C.	simplify	D.	divisible	34.____

Questions 35-43.

DIRECTIONS: Each of Questions 35 to 43 consists of four names. For each question, select the one of the four names that should be FOURTH if the four names were arranged in alphabetical order in accordance with the Rules for Alphabetical Filing given below. Read these rules carefully. Then, for each question, indicate in the correspondingly numbered space at the right the letter preceding the name that should be FOURTH in alphabetical order.

RULES FOR ALPHABETICAL FILING

NAMES OF INDIVIDUALS

(1)   *File all names of individuals in strict alphabetical order, first according to the last name, then according to first name or initial, and finally according to middle name or initial. For example: George Brown precedes Edward Hunt, and Charles N. Smith precedes David A. Smith.*

(2)   *Where the last names are identical, the one with an initial instead of a first name precedes the one with a first name beginning with the same initial. For example: G. Brown and G.B. Brown precede George A. Brown.*

(3)   *Where two identical last names also have identical first names or initials, the one without a middle name or initial precedes the one with a middle name or initial. For example: William Jones precedes both William B. Jones and William Bruce Jones.*

(4)   *When two last names are identical and the two first names or initials are also identical, the one with a middle initial precedes the one with a middle name beginning with the same initial. For example: William B. Jones precedes William Bruce Jones.*

(5)   *Prefixes such as D', De, La, and Le are considered parts of the names they precede. For example: George De Gregory precedes Arthur Dempsey.*

(6)   *Last names beginning with "Mac" or "Mc" are to be filed as spelled.*

(7)   *Abbreviated names are to be treated as if they were spelled out. For example: Chas. is filed as Charles, and Wm. is filed as William.*

(8)   *Titles and designations such as Dr., Mr., and Prof, are to be disregarded in filing.*

NAMES OF BUSINESS ORGANIZATIONS

(1)   File names of business organizations exactly as written, except that an organization bearing the name of an individual is filed alphabetically according to the name of the individual in accordance with the rules for filing names of individuals given above. For example: *Samuel Eartnett Lumber Company* precedes *Mutual Grocery Company*.

(2)   Where numerals occur in a name, they are to be treated as if they were spelled out. For example: *5* stands for *five* and *9th* stands for *ninth*.

(3)   Where the following words occur in names, they are to be disregarded: *the, of, and*.

SAMPLE:

A.	William Brown	(2)
B.	Arthur F. Browne	(4)
C.	Arthur Browne	(3)
D.	F. Brown	(1)

The numbers in parentheses indicate the proper alphabetical order in which these names should be filed. Since the name that should be filed FOURTH is Arthur F. Browne, the answer is B.

35. A. Francis Lattimore   B. H. Latham   35.___
     C. G. Lattimore   D. Hugh Latham

36. A. Thomas B. Morgan   B. Thomas Morgan   36.___
     C. T. Morgan   D. Thomas Bertram Morgan

37. A. Lawrence A. Villon   B. Chas. Valente   37.___
     C. Charles M. Valent   D. Lawrence De Villon

38. A. Alfred Devance   B. A.R. D'Amico   38.___
     C. Arnold De Vincent   D. A. De Pino

39. A. Dr. Milton A. Bergmann   B. Miss Evelyn M. Bergmenn   39.___
     C. Prof. E.N. Bergmenn   D. Mrs. L.B. Bergmann

40. A. George MacDougald   B. Thomas McHern   40.___
     C. William Macholt   D. Frank McHenry

41. A. Third National Bank B. Robt. Tempkin Corp.   41.___
     C. 32nd Street Carpet Co. D. Wm. Templeton, Inc.

42. A. Mary Lobell Art Shop B. John La Marca, Inc.   42.___
     C. Lawyers' Guild   D. Frank Le Goff Studios

43. A. 9th Avenue Garage   B. Jos. Nuren Food Co.   43.___
     C. The New Book Store   D. Novelty Card Corp.

Questions 44-50.

DIRECTIONS: Questions 44 to 50 are to be answered on the basis of the following Code Table. In this table, for each number a corresponding code letter is given. Each of the questions contains three pairs of numbers and code letters. In each pair, the code letters should correspond with the numbers in accordance with the Code Table.

CODE TABLE

Number	1	2	3	4	5	6	7	8	9	0
Corresponding Code Letter	Y	N	Z	X	W	T	U	P	S	R

In some of the pairs below, an error exists in the coding. Examine the pairs in each question carefully.
If an error exists in:
   only one of the pairs in the question, mark your answer A
   any two pairs in the question, mark your answer B all three pairs in the question, mark your answer C none of the pairs in the question, mark your answer D

SAMPLE:

       37258   -   ZUNWP
       948764   -   SXPTTX
       73196   -   UZYSP

In the above sample, the first pair is correct since each number, as listed, has the correct corresponding code letter. In the second pair, an error exists because the number 7 should have the code letter U instead of the letter T. In the third pair, an error exists because the number 6 should have the code letter T instead of the letter P. Since there are errors in two of the three pairs, the correct answer is B.

44.   493785 - XSZUPW   44._____
      86398207 - PTUSPNRU
      5943162 - WSXZYTN

45.   5413968412 - WXYZSTPXYR   45._____
      8763451297 - PUTZXWYZSU
      4781965302 - XUPYSUWZRN

46.   79137584 - USYRUWPX   46._____
      638247 - TZPNXS
      49679312 - XSTUSZYN

47.   37854296 - ZUPWXNST   47._____
      09183298 - RSYXZNSP
      91762358 - SYUTNXWP

48.   3918762485 - ZSYPUTNXPW   48._____
      1578291436 - YWUPNSYXZT
      2791385674 - NUSYZPWTUX

49. 197546821 - YSUWSTPNY
    873024867 - PUZRNWPTU
    583179246 - WPZYURNXT   49._____

50. 510782463 - WYRUSNXTZ
    478192356 - XUPYSNZWT   50._____
    961728532 - STYUNPWXN

———

KEY (CORRECT ANSWERS)

1.	C	11.	D	21.	A	31.	B	41.	C
2.	A	12.	A	22.	D	32.	C	42.	A
3.	B	13.	B	23.	D	33.	D	43.	B
4.	D	14.	A	24.	B	34.	A	44.	A
5.	C	15.	C	25.	B	35.	C	45.	C
6.	B	16.	D	26.	D	36.	D	46.	B
7.	A	17.	A	27.	A	37.	A	47.	B
8.	B	18.	C	28.	C	38.	C	48.	D
9.	D	19.	B	29.	B	39.	B	49.	C
10.	A	20.	A	30.	A	40.	B	50.	B

———

EXAMINATION SECTION
TEST 1

DIRECTIONS: Each question or incomplete statement is followed by several suggested answers or completions. Select the one that BEST answers the question or completes the statement. *PRINT THE LETTER OF THE CORRECT ANSWER IN THE SPACE AT THE RIGHT.*

1. A city agency whose employees come into frequent contact with the public can gain public approval of its work MOST effectively by   1.____

    A. distributing pamphlets describing its objectives and work to the people who come into contact with the agency
    B. encouraging its employees to behave properly when off duty so as to impress the public favorably
    C. making certain that its employees perform their daily services efficiently and courteously
    D. having its officials give lectures to civic groups, describing the agency's efficiency and accomplishments

2. Assume that you are a newly appointed clerk in a city agency. While your superior is at a conference that may last for several hours, a visitor enters the office and asks you for information on certain of your agency's procedures with which you are not familiar.
Of the following, the BEST action for you to take is to   2.____

    A. ask the visitor to return to the office later in the day when your superior will have returned
    B. ask the visitor to wait in the office until your superior returns
    C. ask a more experienced clerk in your office to answer the visitor's questions
    D. advise the visitor that the information that he is seeking will be given to him if he writes to your superior

3. A visitor to an office in a city agency tells one of the clerks that he has an appointment with the supervisor of the office who is expected shortly. The visitor asks for permission to wait in the supervisor's private office, which is unoccupied at the moment.
For the clerk to allow the visitor to do so would be   3.____

    A. *desirable;* the visitor would be less likely to disturb the other employees or to be disturbed by them
    B. *undesirable;* it is not courteous to permit a visitor to be left alone in an office
    C. *desirable;* the supervisor may wish to speak to the visitor in private
    D. *undesirable;* the supervisor may have left confidential papers on his desk

4. Mr. Jones is a clerk in Bureau A in a city agency. Of the following, the MOST appropriate statement for Mr. Jones to make when answering the telephone in his office is   4.____

    A. "Hello. This is Mr. Jones."
    B. "Bureau A, Mr. Jones."
    C. "This is Bureau A. What can we do for you?"
    D. "Bureau A, who is this please?"

5. Your supervisor has given you about two thousand 3x5 cards to arrange in alphabetical order.
   For you first to sort the cards into several broad groups, such as A to E, F to K, etc., and then alphabetize each group of cards separately is

    5.___

   A. *desirable;* proportionately less time is required to sort small groups of cards than large groups of cards
   B. *undesirable;* a process of alphabetizing which requires more than one step wastes too much time
   C. *desirable;* full use can then be made of all information on the cards
   D. *undesirable;* fewer alphabetizing errors will be made in a small group of cards than in a large group of cards

6. A clerk assigned to the mail unit of a city agency has completed his assigned duties for the day about two hours before closing time.
   In this situation, it is MOST advisable for the clerk to

    6.___

   A. do some of his work over again in order to attain greater skill
   B. report to his supervisor that he has completed his assignment
   C. ask the supervisor of an adjoining unit for permission to observe the work of that unit
   D. ask a fellow employee if he would like to have help in completing his work for the day

7. A mail clerk assigned to the task of inserting outgoing letters into envelopes notices that one letter has not been signed.
   The MOST appropriate of the following actions for the clerk to take is to

    7.___

   A. sign the letter with his own name
   B. sign the letter with the dictator's name and his own initials
   C. return the letter to the dictator for signature
   D. mail the letter without the signature

8. The MOST important characteristic of a tickler card file is that the cards are arranged according to

    8.___

   A. subject matter
   B. the date on which action is to be taken
   C. the name of the individual on the card
   D. the order of importance of the items contained on the cards

9. As a clerk in a city department, one of your duties is to maintain the files in your bureau. Material from these files is sometimes used by other bureaus. You frequently find that you are unable to locate some material because it has been removed from the files and is evidently being used by some other bureau.
   The BEST way to correct this situation is to

    9.___

   A. have an out-of-file card filled out and filed whenever material is borrowed from the files
   B. forbid employees of other bureaus to borrow material from the files unless they promise to return it promptly
   C. provide other bureaus with duplicate files
   D. notify your supervisor whenever an employee from another bureau is slow in returning material to the files

10. Assume that you are assigned as stock room clerk in your department.
Of the following practices, the one that would be LEAST advisable for you to follow is that

    A. the supply of an article should be exhausted before a new supply is ordered
    B. articles requested frequently should be stored in a readily available place
    C. units of an article should, in general, be stored so that the oldest is used first
    D. articles should not be issued without a requisition slip

10.____

11. The Post Office prefers that all outgoing addresses be typewritten or in ink, rather than in pencil.
Of the following, the BEST reason for this preference is that

    A. a pencil address may smudge and become illegible
    B. an address which is typewritten or written in ink is neater
    C. the addressee may wish to retain the envelope for his records
    D. unauthorized changes of addresses are discouraged

11.____

12. A city agency that has recently moved to a new address has started a campaign to reduce the wasteful use of supplies. There are on hand about three thousand legal-sized envelopes bearing the old return address.
In view of this conservation policy, the MOST appropriate action to take with the envelopes would be to

    A. send them only to people who know the new address
    B. use them to store small items like clips and rubber bands
    C. use them only for first class mail
    D. block out the old address and stamp in the new one

12.____

13. The abbreviation *Enc.* which sometimes appears on a business letter flush with the left-hand margin and one
or two lines below the line of the signature indicates that

    A. a carbon copy of the letter has been prepared
    B. a prompt reply to the letter is expected
    C. no reply to the letter is necessary
    D. other papers accompany the letter

13.____

14. Assume that you have been instructed to prepare a copy of a statistical table describing your bureau's activities. The BEST method for making certain that no error has been made in preparing the copy is for you to

    A. compare all the totals and subtotals in the two tables, for if they are identical on the two tables, the copy may be assumed to be accurate
    B. spot check the places in the two tables where errors are most likely to occur
    C. have another clerk read the original table aloud to you while you check the copy
    D. request another clerk to prepare a second copy independently and then compare the two copies

14.____

15. A transfer file is used PRIMARILY to   15.____

    A. carry records from one office to another
    B. store inactive records
    C. hold records that are constantly used by more than one bureau of an organization
    D. hold confidential records

16. The usual reason for endorsement of a check is to   16.____

    A. transfer ownership of the check
    B. identify the drawer of the check
    C. indicate that the check is genuine
    D. prevent payment of the check until a specific date

17. An estimate of revenues and expenditures for the next fiscal year prepared by a govern-   17.____
    mental organization or a private firm is called a(n)

    A. budget   B. appropriation   C. voucher   D. inventory

18. It is required that a clerk satisfactorily complete a probationary period before his appoint-   18.____
    ment to a city job is considered permanent.
    Of the following, the BEST reason for this requirement is that

    A. success on one job is a good indication of success in the next higher job
    B. a clerk usually performs his work more efficiently during his probationary period
       than after that period is completed
    C. actual performance on a job is the most valid test of a clerk's ability to do the work
    D. the rating a person receives on a civil service examination is usually just as signifi-
       cant as the efficiency he demonstrates during his probationary period

19. A government agency should have an established practice of disposing of papers, corre-   19.____
    spondence, and records that are no longer of any use.
    Of the following, the LEAST important reason for establishing such a practice is the
    necessity of

    A. conserving space whenever possible
    B. saving time in filing and locating papers
    C. releasing filing equipment for current needs
    D. obtaining income from the sale of the waste paper

20. Since the government can spend only what it obtains from the people and this amount is   20.____
    ultimately limited by their capacity and willingness to pay taxes, it is very important that
    they should be given full information about the work of the government.
    According to this statement,

    A. governmental employees should be trained not only in their own work, but also in
       how to perform the duties of other employees in their agency
    B. taxation by the government rests upon the consent of the people
    C. the release of full information on the work of the government will increase the effi-
       ciency of governmental operations
    D. the work of the government, in recent years, has been restricted because of
       reduced tax collections

Questions 21-23.

DIRECTIONS: Questions 21 to 23 are to be answered SOLELY on the information contained in the following statement.

The equipment in a mail room may include a mail metering machine. This machine simultaneously stamps, postmarks, seals, and counts letters as fast as the operator can feed them. It can also print the proper postage directly on a gummed strip to be affixed to bulky items. It is equipped with a meter which is removed from the machine and sent to the post-master to be set for a given number of stampings of any denomination. The setting of the meter must be paid for in advance. One of the advantages of metered mail is that it by-passes the cancellation operation and thereby facilitates handling by the post office. Mail metering also makes the pilfering of stamps impossible, but does not prevent the passage of personal mail in company envelopes through the meters unless there is established a rigid control or censorship over outgoing mail.

21.   According to this statement, the postmaster   21.____

    A.   is responsible for training new clerks in the use of mail metering machines
    B.   usually recommends that both large and small firms adopt the use of mail metering machines
    C.   is responsible for setting the meter to print a fixed number of stampings
    D.   examines the mail metering machines to see that they are properly installed in the mail room

22.   According to this statement, the use of mail metering machines   22.____

    A.   requires the employment of more clerks in a mail room than does the use of post-age stamps
    B.   interferes with the handling of large quantities of outgoing mail
    C.   does not prevent employees from sending their personal letters at company expense
    D.   usually involves smaller expenditures for mail room equipment than does the use of postage stamps

23.   On the basis of this statement, it is MOST accurate to state that   23.____

    A.   mail metering machines are often used for opening envelopes
    B.   postage stamps are generally used when bulky packages are to be mailed
    C.   the use of metered mail tends to interfere with rapid mail handling by the post office
    D.   mail metering machines can seal and count letters at the same time

Questions 24-25.

DIRECTIONS: Questions 24 and 25 are to be answered SOLELY on the basis of the information contained in the following statement.

Forms are printed sheets of paper on which information is to be entered. While what is printed on the form is most important, the kind of paper used in making the form is also important. The kind of paper should be selected with regard to the use to which the form will be subjected. Printing a form on an unnecessarily expensive grade of papers is wasteful. On the other hand, using too cheap or flimsy a form can materially interfere with satisfactory performance of the work the form is being planned to do. Thus, a form printed on both sides normally requires a heavier paper than a form printed only on one side. Forms to be used as permanent records, or which are expected to have a very long life in files, require a quality of paper which will not disintegrate or discolor with age. A form which will go through a great deal of handling requires a strong tough paper, while thinness is a necessary qualification where the making of several copies of a form will be required.

24. According to this statement, the type of paper used for making forms

    A. should be chosen in accordance with the use to which the form will be put
    B. should be chosen before the type of printing to be used has been decided upon
    C. is as important as the information which is printed on it
    D. should be strong enough to be used for any purpose

24.____

25. According to this statement, forms that are

    A. printed on both sides are usually economical and desirable
    B. to be filed permanently should not deteriorate as time goes on
    C. expected to last for a long time should be handled carefully
    D. to be filed should not be printed on inexpensive paper

25.____

26. The CHIEF purpose of assessing real estate each year is to determine

    A. the amount of real estate tax that the owner must pay
    B. the value of unused real estate in the city
    C. the improvements that the owner must make in his property
    D. how the property is being used

26.____

27. Certain types of local laws are submitted to the voters for approval. The submission of these laws to the voters for approval is known as

    A. the initiative
    C. the referendum
    B. proportional representation
    D. eminent domain

27.____

28. A new alphabetical name card file covering fifteen file drawers has been set up in your office. Your supervisor asks you to place identifying labels outside each file drawer. Of the following, the BEST rule for you to follow in determining the appropriate label for each drawer is that

    A. the alphabet should be divided equally among the file drawers available
    B. each label should give the beginning and ending points of the cards in that drawer
    C. each drawer should begin with a new letter of the alphabet
    D. no drawer should contain more than two letters of the alphabet

28.____

29. One of the administrators in your department cannot find an important letter left on his desk. He believes that the letter may accidentally have been placed among a group of letters sent to you for filing. You look in the file and find the letter filed in its correct place. Of the following, the BEST suggestion for you to make to your supervisor in order to avoid repetition of such incidents is that

    A. file clerks should be permitted to read material they are requested to file
    B. correspondence files should be cross-indexed
    C. a periodic check should be made of the files to locate material inaccurately filed
    D. material which is sent to the file clerk should be marked *O.K. for filing*

29.____

30. One of your duties is to keep a file of administrative orders by date. Your supervisor often asks you to find the order concerning a particular subject. Since you are rarely able to remember the date of the order, it is necessary for you to search through the entire file. Of the following, the BEST suggestion for you to make to your supervisor for remedying this situation is that

    A. each order bear conspicuously in its upper left-hand corner the precise date on which it is issued
    B. old orders be taken from the file and destroyed as soon as they are superseded by new orders, so that the file will not be overcrowded
    C. an alphabetic subject index of orders be prepared so that orders can be located easily by content as well as date
    D. dates be eliminated entirely from orders

30.____

31. Suppose that a fixed number of entries must be made on record cards each month. Because of military leaves, the number of clerks assigned to this work has been reduced by 20 percent over last year, although the total number of entries made remains the same.
Of the following, the MOST accurate statement is that, as compared with last year, the average number of entries now made by each clerk has

    A. remained the same
    B. increased 20 percent
    C. decreased 20 percent
    D. increased 25 percent

31.____

32. Suppose that the employees in your department are classified in five age groups. Your supervisor asks you to find the percentage of employees in each of the five age groups. Of the following, the BEST method to employ for checking the accuracy of your arithmetic in computing the percentages is to

    A. arrange the five percentages in increasing order of magnitude
    B. reduce the five percentages to common terms
    C. add the five percentages
    D. divide each percentage by the total number of individuals in that age group

32.____

33. Suppose that you are newly assigned to a large office in your department. You believe that a certain change in office routine would be desirable.
Of the following, the BEST reason for suggesting this modification to your supervisor is that

    A. even good supervisors are sometimes reluctant to institute innovations
    B. your suggestion may result in the saving of considerable time and money
    C. major changes in office routine are easier to make in small offices than in large offices
    D. a new employee will usually be able to think of new ways of doing his work

33.____

34. A clerk divided his 35-hour work week as follows:
1/5 of his time in sorting mail;
1/2 of his time in filing letters; and
1/7 of his time in reception work.
The rest of his time was devoted to messenger work. The percentage of time spent on messenger work by the clerk during the week was MOST NEARLY

    A. 6%   B. 10%   C. 14%   D. 16%

34.____

35. A city department has set up a computing unit and has rented 5 computing machines at a monthly rental of $140 per machine. In addition, the cost to the department for the maintenance and repair of each of these machines is $10 per month. Five computing machine operators, each receiving a monthly salary of $3,000, and a supervisor, who receives $3,800 a month, have been assigned to this unit. This unit will perform the work previously performed by 10 employees whose combined salary was $32,400 a month. On the basis of these facts, the savings that will result from the operation of this computing unit for 5 months will be MOST NEARLY   35.____

    A. $50,000   B. $64,000   C. $66,000   D. $95,000

36. Twelve clerks are assigned to enter certain data on index cards. This number of clerks could perform the task in 18 days. After these clerks have worked on this assignment for 6 days, 4 more clerks are added to the staff to do this work.
Assuming that all the clerks work at the same rate of speed, the entire task, instead of taking 18 days, will be performed in _____ days.   36.____

    A. 9   B. 12   C. 15   D. 16

Questions 37-50.

DIRECTIONS: Each of Questions 37 to 50 consists of a word in capitals followed by four suggested meanings of the word. Print in the correspondingly numbered space at the right the letter preceding the word which means MOST NEARLY the same as the word in capitals.

37. FUNDAMENTAL   37.____
    A. adequate   B. essential   C. official   D. truthful

38. SUPPLANT   38.____
    A. approve   B. displace   C. satisfy   D. vary

39. OBLITERATE   39.____
    A. erase   B. demonstrate   C. review   D. detect

40. ANTICIPATE   40.____
    A. foresee   B. approve   C. annul   D. conceal

41. EXORBITANT   41.____
    A. priceless   B. extensive   C. worthless   D. excessive

42. RELUCTANT   42.____
    A. anxious   B. constant   C. drastic   D. hesitant

43. PREVALENT   43.____
    A. current   B. permanent   C. durable   D. temporary

44. AUGMENT   44.____
    A. conclude   B. suggest   C. increase   D. unite

45. FRUGAL   45.____
    A. friendly   B. thoughtful   C. hostile   D. economica ✓

46. AUSTERITY   46.____
    A. priority   B. severity   C. anxiety   D. solitude

47. CORROBORATION   47.____
    A. expenditure   B. compilation   C. confirmation   D. reduction

48. IMPERATIVE   48.____
    A. impending   B. impossible   C. compulsory   D. logical

49. FEASIBLE   49.____
    A. simple   B. practicable ✓   C. visible   D. lenient

50. SALUTARY   50.____
    A. popular   B. urgent   C. beneficial   D. forceful

_____

KEY (CORRECT ANSWER)

1.	C	11.	A	21.	C	31.	D	41.	D
2.	C	12.	D	22.	C	32.	C	42.	D
3.	D	13.	D	23.	D	33.	B	43.	A
4.	B	14.	C	24.	A	34.	D	44.	C
5.	A	15.	B	25.	B	35.	B	45.	D
6.	B	16.	A	26.	A	36.	C	46.	B
7.	C	17.	A	27.	C	37.	B	47.	C
8.	B	18.	C	28.	B	38.	B	48.	C
9.	A	19.	D	29.	B	39.	A	49.	B
10.	A	20.	B	30.	C	40.	A	50.	C

_____

TEST 2

DIRECTIONS: Each of Questions 1 to 2 consists of a word in capitals followed by four suggested meanings of the word. Print in the correspondingly numbered space at the right the letter preceding the word which means MOST NEARLY the same as the word in capitals.

1. ACQUIESCE   1.____

    A. endeavor   B. discharge   C. agree   D. inquire

2. DIFFIDENCE   2.____

    A. shyness   B. distinction   C. interval   D. discordance

Questions 3-17.

DIRECTIONS: Each of Questions 3 to 17 consists of a sentence which may be classified appropriately under one of the following four categories:
    A.   incorrect because of faulty grammar or sentence structure
    B.   incorrect because of faulty punctuation
    C.   incorrect because of faulty capitalization
    D.   correct

Examine each sentence carefully. Then, in the correspondingly numbered space at the right, print the letter preceding the option which is the BEST of the four suggested above. All incorrect sentences contain only one type of error. Consider a sentence correct if it contains none of the types of errors mentioned, although there may be other correct ways of expressing the same thought.

3. Mrs. Black the supervisor of the unit, has many important duties.   3.____

4. We spoke to the man whom you saw yesterday.   4.____

5. When a holiday falls on Sunday, it is officially celebrated on monday.   5.____

6. Of the two reports submitted, this one is the best.   6.____

7. Each staff member, including the accountants, were invited to the meeting.   7.____

8. Give the package to whomever calls for it.   8.____

9. To plan the work is our responsibility; to carry it out is his.   9.____

10. "May I see the person in charge of this office," asked the visitor?   10.____

11. He knows that it was not us who prepared the report.   11.____

12. These problems were brought to the attention of senator Johnson.   12.____

13. The librarian classifies all books periodicals and documents.   13.____

14. Any employee who uses an adding machine realizes its importance.   14.____

15. Instead of coming to the office, the clerk should of come to the supply room.   15.____

16. He asked, "will your staff assist us?" 16.____

17. Having been posted on the bulletin board, we were certain that the announcements would be read. 17.____

Questions 18-27.

DIRECTIONS: Each of Questions 18 to 27 consists of a group of four words. One word in each group is INCORRECTLY spelled. For each question, print in the correspondingly numbered space at the right the letter preceding the word which is INCORRECTLY spelled.

18.	A. typical	B. descend	C. summarize	D. continuel	18.____
19.	A. courageous	B. recomend	C. omission	D. eliminate	19.____
20.	A. compliment	B. illuminate	C. auxilary	D. installation	20.____
21.	A. preliminary	B. aquainted	C. syllable	D. analysis	21.____
22.	A. accustomed	B. negligible	C. interupted	D. bulletin	22.____
23.	A. summoned	B. managment	C. mechanism	D. sequence	23.____
24.	A. commitee	B. surprise	C. noticeable	D. emphasize	24.____
25.	A. occurrance	B. likely	C. accumulate	D. grievance	25.____
26.	A. obstacle	B. particuliar	C. baggage	D. fascinating	26.____
27.	A. innumerable	B. seize	C. applicant	D. dictionery	27.____

Questions 28-37.

DIRECTIONS: Each of Questions 28 to 37 consists of four names grouped vertically under four different filing arrangements lettered A, B, C, and D. In each question, only one of the four arrangements lists the names in the correct filing order according to the Rules for Alphabetical Filing given below. Read these rules carefully. Then, for each question, select the CORRECT filing arrangement, lettered A, B, C, or D and print in the appropriately numbered space at the right the letter of that CORRECT filing arrangement.

RULES FOR ALPHABETICAL FILING

NAMES OF INDIVIDUALS

(1) File all names of individuals in strict alphabetical order, first according to the last name, then according to first name or initial, and finally according to middle name or initial. For example: Robert Stone precedes Arnold Taft, and Edward H. Stone precedes G.A. Stone.

(2) Where the last names are identical, the one with an initial instead of a first name precedes the one with a first name beginning with the same initial. For example: R. Stone and R.B. Stone precede Robert Stone.

(3) Where two identical last names also have identical first names or initials, the one without a middle name or initial precedes the one with a middle name or initial. For example: R. Stone precedes R.B. Stone, and Robert Stone precedes Robert B. Stone.

(4) Where two identical last names also have identical first names or initials, the one with an initial instead of a middle name precedes the one with a middle name beginning with the same initial. For example: Robert B. Stone precedes Robert Burton Stone.

(5) Prefixes such as De, La, Le, and O' are considered as part of the names they precede. For example: John De Solle precedes Arthur Dexter.

(6) Names beginning with "Mac" and "Mc" are to be filed as spelled.

(7) Abbreviated names are to be treated as if they were spelled out. For example: Chas. stands for Charles, and Wm. stands for William.

(8) Titles and designations such as Dr., Mr., and Prof. are to be disregarded in filing.

NAMES OF BUSINESS ORGANIZATIONS

(1) File names of business organizations exactly as written, except that an organization bearing the name of an individual is filed alphabetically according to the name of the individual with the rules for filing names of individuals given above. For example: Thomas Miller Paper Co. precedes National Lumber Co.

(2) Where numerals occur in a name, they are to be treated as if they were spelled out. For example: 4 stands for four, and 8th stands for eighth.

(3) Where the following words occur in names, they are to be disregarded: the, of, and.

SAMPLE:

ARRANGEMENT A	ARRANGEMENT B	ARRANGEMENT C	ARRANGEMENT D
Arnold Robinson	Arthur Roberts	Arnold Robinson	Arthur Roberts
Arthur Roberts	J.B. Robin	Arthur Roberts	James Robin
J.B. Robin	James Robin	James Robin	J.B. Robin
James Robin	Arnold Robinson	J.B. Robin	Arnold Robinson

Since, in this sample, ARRANGEMENT B is the only one in which the four names are correctly arranged alphabetically, the answer is B.

28.   ARRANGEMENT A   ARRANGEMENT B   28.____
       Alice Thompson   Eugene Thompkins
       Arnold G. Thomas   Alice Thompson
       B. Thomas   Arnold G. Thomas
       Eugene Thompkins   B. Thomas

ARRANGEMENT <u>C</u>
B. Thomas
Arnold G. Thomas
Eugene Thompkins
Alice Thompson

ARRANGEMENT <u>D</u>
Arnold G. Thomas
B. Thomas
Eugene Thompkins
Alice Thompson

29. ARRANGEMENT <u>A</u>
Albert Green
A.B. Green
Frank E. Green
Wm. Greenfield

ARRANGEMENT <u>B</u>
A.B. Green
Albert Green
Frank E. Green
Wm. Greenfield

29.____

ARRANGEMENT <u>C</u>
Albert Green
Wm. Greenfield
A.B. Green
Frank E. Green

ARRANGEMENT <u>D</u>
A.B. Green
Frank E. Green
Albert Green
Wm. Greenfield

30. ARRANGEMENT <u>A</u>
Steven M. Comte
Robt. Count
Robert B. Count
Steven Le Comte

ARRANGEMENT <u>B</u>
Steven Le Comte
Steven M. Comte
Robert B. Count
Robt. Count

30.____

ARRANGEMENT <u>C</u>
Steven M. Comte
Steven Le Comte
Robt. Count
Robert B. Count

ARRANGEMENT <u>D</u>
Robt. Count
Robert B. Count
Steven Le Comte
Steven M. Comte

31. ARRANGEMENT <u>A</u>
Prof. David Towner
Miss Edna Tower
Dr. Frank I. Tower
Mrs. K.C. Towner

ARRANGEMENT <u>B</u>
Dr. Frank I. Tower
Miss Edna Tower
Mrs. K.C. Towner
Prof. David Towner

31.____

ARRANGEMENT <u>C</u>
Miss Edna Tower
Dr. Frank I. Tower
Prof. David Towner
Mrs. K.C. Towner

ARRANGEMENT <u>D</u>
Prof. David Towner
Mrs. K.C. Towner
Miss Edna Tower
Dr. Frank I. Tower

32. ARRANGEMENT <u>A</u>
The Jane Miller Shop
Joseph Millard Corp.
John Muller & Co.
Jean Mullins, Inc.

ARRANGEMENT <u>B</u>
Joseph Millard Corp.
The Jane Miller Shop
John Muller & Co.
Jean Mullins, Inc.

32.____

ARRANGEMENT <u>C</u>
The Jane Miller Shop
Jean Mullins, Inc.
John Muller & Co.
Joseph Millard Corp.

ARRANGEMENT <u>D</u>
Joseph Millard Corp.
John Muller & Co.
Jean Mullins, Inc.
The Jane Miller Shop

33.

ARRANGEMENT A
Anthony Delaney
A.M. D'Elia
A. De Landri
Alfred De Monte

ARRANGEMENT C
A. De Landri
A.M. D'Elia
Alfred De Monte
Anthony Delaney

ARRANGEMENT B
Anthony Delaney
A. De Landri
A.M. D'Elia
Alfred De Monte

ARRANGEMENT D
A. De Landri
Anthony Delaney
A.M. D'Elia
Alfred De Monte

33.____

34.

ARRANGEMENT A
D. McAllen
Lewis McBride
Doris MacAllister
Lewis T. MacBride

ARRANGEMENT C
Doris MacAllister
Lewis T. MacBride
D. McAllen
Lewis McBride

ARRANGEMENT B
D. McAllen
Doris MacAllister
Lewis McBride
Lewis T. MacBride

ARRANGEMENT D
Doris MacAllister
D. McAllen
Lewis T. MacBride
Lewis McBride

34.____

35.

ARRANGEMENT A
6th Ave. Swim Shop
The Sky Ski School
Sport Shoe Store
23rd Street Salon

ARRANGEMENT C
6th Ave. Swim Shop
Sport Shoe Store
The Sky Ski School
23rd Street Salon

ARRANGEMENT B
23rd Street Salon
The Sky Ski School
6th Ave. Swim Shop
Sport Shoe Store

ARRANGEMENT D
The Sky Ski School
6th Ave. Swim Shop
Sport Shoe Store
23rd Street Salon

35.____

36.

ARRANGEMENT A
Charlotte Stair
C.B. Stare
Charles B. Stare
Elaine La Stella

ARRANGEMENT C
Elaine La Stella
Charlotte Stair
C.B. Stare
Charles B. Stare

ARRANGEMENT B
C.B. Stare
Charles B. Stare
Charlotte Stair
Elaine La Stella

ARRANGEMENT D
Charles B. Stare
C.B. Stare
Charlotte Stair
Elaine La Stella

36.____

37.

ARRANGEMENT A	ARRANGEMENT B
John O'Farrell Corp.	Finest Glass Co.
Finest Glass Co.	4th Guarantee Bank
George Fraser Co.	George Fraser Co.
4th Guarantee Bank	John O'Farrell Corp.

ARRANGEMENT C	ARRANGEMENT D
John O'Farrell Corp.	Finest Glass Co.
Finest Glass Co.	George Fraser Co.
4th Guarantee Bank	John O'Farrell Corp.
George Fraser Co.	4th Guarantee Bank

37.____

Questions 38-47.

DIRECTIONS: Questions 38 to 47 are based on the Weekly Payroll Record, shown below, of Bureau X in a public agency. In answering these questions, note that gross weekly salary is the salary before deductions have been made; take-home pay is the amount remaining after all indicated weekly deductions have been made from the gross weekly salary. In answering questions involving annual amounts, compute on the basis of 52 weeks per year.

BUREAU X
WEEKLY PAYROLL PERIOD

Unit in Which Employed	Employee	Title	Gross Weekly Salary (Before Deductions)	Medical Insurance	Income Tax	Pension System
Accounting	Allen	Accountant	$950	$14.50	$125.00	$53.20
"	Earth	Bookkeeper	720	19.00	62.00	40.70
"	Keller	Clerk	580	6.50	82.00	33.10
"	Peters	Typist	560	6.50	79.00	35.30
"	Simons	Stenographer	610	14.50	64.00	37.80
Information	Brown	Clerk	560	13.00	56.00	42.22
"	Smith	Clerk	590	14.50	61.00	58.40
"	Turner	Typist	580	13.00	59.00	62.60
"	Williams	Stenographer	620	19.00	44.00	69.40
Mail	Conner	Clerk	660	13.00	74.00	55.40
"	Farrell	Typist	540	6.50	75.00	34.00
"	Johnson	Stenographer	580	19.00	36.00	37.10
Records	Dillon	Clerk	640	6.50	94.00	58.20
"	Martin	Clerk	540	19.00	29.00	50.20
"	Standish	Typist	620	14.50	67.00	60.10
"	Wilson	Stenographer	690	6.50	101.00	75.60

38.   Dillon's annual take-home pay is MOST NEARLY

38.____

   A. $25,000   B. $27,000   C. $31,000   D. $33,000

39. The difference between Turner's gross annual salary and his annual take-home pay is MOST NEARLY

    A. $3,000   B. $5,000   C. $7,000   D. $9,000

39.____

40. Of the following, the employee whose weekly take-home pay is CLOSEST to that of Keller's is

    A. Peters   B. Brown   C. Smith   D. Turner

40.____

41. The average gross annual salary of the typists is

    A. less than $27,500
    B. more than $27,500 but less than $30,000
    C. more than $30,000 but less than $32,500
    D. more than $32,500

41.____

42. The average gross weekly salary of the stenographers EXCEEDS the gross weekly salary of the clerks by

    A. $20   B. $30   C. $40   D. $50

42.____

43. Of the following employees in the Accounting Unit, the one who pays the HIGHEST percentage of his gross weekly salary for the Pension System is

    A. Barth   B. Keller   C. Peters   D. Simons

43.____

44. For all of the Accounting Unit employees, the total annual deductions for Medical Insurance are less than the total annual deductions for the Pension System by MOST NEARLY

    A. $6,000   B. $7,000   C. $8,000   D. $9,000

44.____

45. Of the following, the employee whose total weekly deductions are MOST NEARLY 27% of his gross weekly salary is

    A. Barth   B. Brown   C. Martin   D. Wilson

45.____

46. The total amount of the gross weekly salaries of all the employees in the Records Unit is MOST NEARLY

    A. 95% of the total amount of the gross weekly salaries of all the employees in the Information Unit
    B. 10% greater than the total amount of the gross weekly salaries of all the employees in the Mail Unit
    C. 75% of the total amount of the gross weekly salaries of all the employees in the Accounting Unit
    D. four times as great as the total amount deducted weekly for tax for all the employees in the Records Unit

46.____

47. For the employees in the Information Unit, the average weekly deductions for Income Tax   47._____

    A. exceeds the average weekly deduction for Income Tax for the employees in the Records Unit
    B. is less than the average weekly deduction for the Pension System for the employees in the Mail Unit
    C. exceeds the average weekly deduction for Income Tax for the employees in the Accounting Unit
    D. is less than the average weekly deduction for the Pension System for the employees in the Records Unit

Questions 48-50.

DIRECTIONS: Questions 48 to 50 are a test of your proofreading ability. Each question consists of Copy I and Copy II. You are to assume that Copy I in each question is correct. Copy II, which is meant to be a duplicate of Copy I, may contain some typographical errors. In each question, compare Copy II with Copy I and determine the number of errors in Copy II. If there are:
      no errors, mark your answer A;
      1 or 2 errors, mark your answer B;
      3 or 4 errors, mark your answer C;
      5 errors or more, mark your answer D.

48. <u>COPY I</u>   48._____
It shall be unlawful to install wires or appliances for electric light, heat or power, operating at a potential in excess of seven hundred fifty volts, in or on any part of a building, with the exception of a central station, sub-station, transformer, or switching vault, or motor room; provided, however, that the Commissioner may authorize the use of radio transmitting apparatus under special conditions.

<u>COPY II</u>
It shall be unlawful to install wires or appliances for electric light, heat or power, operating at a potential in excess of seven hundred fifty volts, in or on any part of a building, with the exception of a central station, substation, transformer, or switching vault, or motor room, provided, however, that the Commissioner may authorize the use of radio transmitting apparatus under special conditions.

49. <u>COPY I</u>   49._____
The grand total debt service for the fiscal year 2006-07 amounts to $350,563,718.63, as compared with $309,561,347.27 for the current fiscal year, or an increase of $41,002,371.36. The amount payable from other sources in 2006-07 shows an increase of $13,264,165.47, resulting in an increase of $27,733,205.89 payable from tax levy funds.

<u>COPY II</u>
The grand total debt service for the fiscal year 2006-07 amounts to $350,568,718.63, as compared with $309,561,347.27 for the current fiscel year, or an increase of $41,002.371.36. The amount payable from other sources in 2006-07 show an increase of $13,264,165.47 resulting in an increase of $27,733,295.89 payable from tax levy funds.

50. <u>COPY I</u>   50.____

The following site proposed for the new building is approximately rectangular in shape and comprises an entire block, having frontages of about 721 feet on 16th Road, 200 feet on 157th Street, 721 feet on 17th Avenue and 200 feet on 154th Street, with a gross area of about 144,350 square feet. The 2006-07 assessed valuation is $28,700 of which $6,000 is for improvements.

<u>COPY II</u>

The following site proposed for the new building is approximetely rectangular in shape and comprises an entire block, having frontage of about 721 feet on 16th Road, 200 feet on 157th Street, 721 feet on 17th Avenue, and 200 feet on 134th Street, with a gross area of about 114,350 square feet. The 2006-07 assessed valuation is $28,700 of which $6,000 is for improvements.

———

KEY (CORRECT ANSWERS)

1. C	11. A	21. B	31. C	41. B
2. A	12. C	22. C	32. B	42. B
3. B	13. B	23. B	33. D	43. C
4. D	14. D	24. A	34. C	44. B
5. C	15. A	25. A	35. A	45. D
6. A	16. C	26. B	36. C	46. C
7. A	17. A	27. D	37. B	47. D
8. A	18. D	28. D	38. A	48. C
9. D	19. B	29. B	39. C	49. D
10. B	20. C	30. A	40. C	50. D

———

EXAMINATION SECTION
TEST 1

DIRECTIONS: Each question or incomplete statement is followed by several suggested answers or completions. Select the one that BEST answers the question or completes the statement. *PRINT THE LETTER OF THE CORRECT ANSWER IN THE SPACE AT THE RIGHT.*

1. A city employee should realize that in his contacts with the public,   1.____

    A. he should always agree with what a visitor says because *the customer is always right*
    B. he should not give any information over the telephone unless the caller identifies himself
    C. the manner in which he treats a visitor may determine the visitor's opinion of government employees generally
    D. visitors should at all times be furnished with all the information they request

2. The one of the following that is LEAST useful to a clerk employed in the mail unit of a large city department is knowing the   2.____

    A. functions of the various divisions in the department
    B. names of the various division heads
    C. location of the various divisions
    D. salaries of the various division heads

3. A clerk notices that a visitor has just entered the office. The other clerks are not aware of the visitor's presence. The MOST appropriate of the following actions for the clerk to take is to   3.____

    A. attend to the visitor immediately
    B. continue with his own work and leave the handling of the visitor to one of the other clerks
    C. cough loudly to direct the attention of the other clerks to the presence of the visitor
    D. continue with his work unless the visitor addresses him directly

4. When a record is borrowed from the files, the file clerk puts a substitution or *out* card in its place.
Of the following, the information that is LEAST commonly placed on the *out* card is   4.____

    A. who borrowed the record
    B. when the record was borrowed
    C. why the record was borrowed
    D. what record was borrowed

5. Of the following, the BEST method of maintaining a mailing list that is subject to frequent changes is to keep the names in a   5.____

    A. loose-leaf address book in which twenty names are entered on each page
    B. card file in which each name is entered on a separate card
    C. bound address book in which twenty-five names are entered on each page
    D. card file in which ten names are entered on each card

6. Of the following, the MAIN reason for using window envelopes instead of plain envelopes in mailing correspondence is that   6._____

    A. window envelopes cost less
    B. the address is less likely to be defaced during delivery
    C. addressing the envelopes is eliminated
    D. the postal rate for window envelopes is less

7. It is frequently helpful to file material under two subjects. In such a case, the material is filed under one subject and a card indicating where the material is filed is placed under the other subject.
This card is known GENERALLY as a _____ card.   7._____

    A. follow-up or tickler
    B. guide
    C. transfer
    D. cross-reference

8. In taking down a telephone message for an employee who is absent from the office, a clerk should consider it LEAST important to indicate in his note to the absent employee the   8._____

    A. time the call was received
    B. number of the telephone extension on which the call came in
    C. name of the clerk who took the message
    D. caller's telephone number

9. A mail clerk whose supervisor has instructed him to send certain items by *parcel post* should send them by   9._____

    A. fourth-class mail
    B. Railway Express
    C. registered first class mail
    D. second-class mail

10. Of the following, the MOST appropriate greeting for a receptionist to use in addressing visitors is   10._____

    A. "Please state your business."
    B. "May I help you?"
    C. "Hello. What is your problem?"
    D. "Do you wish to see someone?"

11. A clerk assigned to the task of adding several long columns of figures performs this work on an adding machine that prints the figures on a paper tape.
In general, the MOST efficient of the following methods of checking the accuracy of the computations is for the clerk to   11._____

    A. check the figures on the paper tape against the corresponding figures in the original material
    B. repeat the computations on the adding machine, using the figures appearing on the paper tape, and then check to see whether the totals on the two tapes are the same
    C. perform the computations manually and check the totals thus obtained against the totals obtained by machine operation
    D. have another clerk repeat the computations manually and check the totals obtained in these two sets of computations

12. The term *via* means MOST NEARLY   12._____

    A. by way of   B. face to face
    C. return postage guaranteed   D. value indicated above

13. A clerk assigned to open and sort incoming mail notices that an envelope does not con-   13._____
tain the enclosure referred to in the letter.
The MOST appropriate of the following actions for him to take is to

    A. delay the delivery of the letter for one day since the enclosure may turn up in the
       next day's mail
    B. forward the letter to the person to whom it is addressed with an indication that the
       enclosure was omitted
    C. forward the letter to the person to whom it is addressed and send a tracer inquiry to
       the post office
    D. return the letter to the writer with a request for the enclosure mentioned in the letter

14. To obtain MOST quickly the telephone number of the General Post Office in the tele-   14._____
phone directory, one should look FIRST under the listing

    A. General Post Office   B. Federal Government
    C. United States Government   D. Post Office Department

15. While your supervisor is at lunch, a visitor approaches you and asks for information   15._____
regarding an important matter. Although you have no information about the matter, you
know that your supervisor has just received a confidential report on the subject and that
the report is still in your supervisor's desk.
The MOST appropriate of the following actions for you to take is to

    A. obtain the report from your supervisor's desk and permit the visitor to read it in
       your presence
    B. tell the visitor that your supervisor has just received a report on this matter and
       suggest that the visitor ask your supervisor for permission to read it
    C. inform the visitor that you have no information on the matter and suggest that he
       return later when the supervisor will be back from lunch
    D. obtain the report from your supervisor's desk and answer the visitor's questions
       from information contained in the report

16. The two sets of initials that are usually placed on the bottom of a business letter flush   16._____
with the left-hand margin and on a line with the last line of the signature indicate

    A. where the letter should be filed
    B. who dictated the letter and who typed it
    C. which persons received copies of the letter
    D. how the letter should be routed

17. When payment of the personal check of a depositor is guaranteed by his bank, that   17._____
check is called a

    A. bank draft   B. voucher check
    C. cashier's check   D. certified check

18. The *Ditto* machine is a(n) _____ machine.   18._____

    A. duplicating   B. transcribing
    C. dictating   D. adding

19. The classified telephone directory is known GENERALLY as The   19.____

   A. Consumers' Buying Guide   B. Business Index
   C. Red Book   D. Commodity Exchange

20. Department X employs 500 men who work in 20 different skilled trades. These men are   20.____
    paid at an hourly rate which differs for each skilled trade. They are paid weekly. The num-
    ber of hours worked by a man varies from week to week. The timekeeping clerk com-
    putes the number of hours a week worked by each man, and the following devices that
    may be used each week to determine the weekly earnings of each of these 500 men, the
    one that will be MOST helpful to the payroll clerk, is a

   A. listing type of adding machine
   B. non-listing type of adding machine
   C. graph showing the average number of hours worked and the average hourly rate of
       pay for each week of the previous year
   D. table listing the amounts obtained by multiplying hourly rates of pay by number of
       hours worked

21. A cash fund kept on hand for the payment of minor office expenses is known GENER-   21.____
    ALLY as

   A. petty cash   B. a sinking fund
   C. a drawing account   D. net assets

22. The term that describes the connection between the inter-office computer technology is   22.____

   A. interface   B. network
   C. hardware   D. software

23. Complaints from the public are no longer regarded by government officials as mere nui-   23.____
    sances. Instead, complaints are often welcomed because they frequently bring into the
    open conditions and faults in operation and service which should be corrected.
    This statement means MOST NEARLY that

   A. government officials now realize that complaints from the public are necessary
   B. faulty operations and services are not brought into the open except by complaints
       from the public
   C. government officials now realize that complaints from the public are in reality a sign
       of a well-run organization
   D. complaints from the public can be useful in indicating needs for improvement in
       operation and service

Questions 24-26.

DIRECTIONS: Questions 24 to 26 are to be answered SOLELY on the basis of the informa-
              tion contained in the following statement.

*The most important unit of the mimeograph machine is a perforated metal drum over
which is stretched a cloth ink pad. A reservoir inside the drum contains the ink which flows
through the perforations and saturates the ink pad. To operate the machine, the operator first
removes from the machine the protective sheet, which keeps the ink from drying while the
machine is not in use. He then hooks the stencil face down on the drum, draws the stencil*

smoothly over the drum, and fastens the stencil at the bottom. The speed with which the drum turns determines the blackness of the copies printed. Slow turning gives heavy, black copies; fast turning gives light, clear-cut reproductions. If reproductions are run on other than porous paper, slip-sheeting is necessary to prevent smearing. Often the printed copy fails to drop readily as it comes from the machine. This may be due to static electricity. To remedy this difficulty, the operator fastens a strip of tinsel from side to side near the impression roller so that the printed copy just touches the soft stems of the tinsel as it is ejected from the machine, thus grounding the static electricity to the frame of the machine.

24. According to this statement,   24._____

    A. turning the drum fast produces light copies
    B. stencils should be placed face up on the drum
    C. ink pads should be changed daily
    D. slip-sheeting is necessary when porous paper is being used

25. According to this statement, when a mimeograph machine is not in use, the   25._____

    A. ink should be drained from the drum
    B. ink pad should be removed
    C. machine should be covered with a protective sheet
    D. counter should be set at zero

26. According to this statement, static electricity is grounded to the frame of the mimeograph   26._____
machine by means of

    A. a slip-sheeting device
    B. a strip of tinsel
    C. an impression roller
    D. hooks located at the top of the drum

Questions 27-28.

DIRECTIONS: Questions 27 and 28 are to be answered SOLELY on the basis of the information contained in the following statement.

The proofreading of material typed from copy is performed more accurately and more speedily when two persons perform this work as a team. The person who did not do the typing should read aloud the original copy while the person who did the typing should check the reading against the typed copy. The reader should speak very slowly and repeat the figures, using a different grouping of numbers when repeating the figures. For example, in reading 1967, the reader may say 'one-nine-six-seven' on first reading the figure and 'nineteen-sixty-seven' on repeating the figure. The reader should read all punctuation marks, taking nothing for granted. Since mistakes can occur anywhere, everything typed should be proofread. To avoid confusion, the proofreading team should use the standard proofreading marks, which are given in most dictionaries.

27. According to this statement,   27.____

    A. the person who holds the typed copy is called the reader
    B. the two members of a proofreading team should take turns in reading the typed copy aloud
    C. the typed copy should be checked by the person who did the typing
    D. the person who did not do the typing should read aloud from the typed copy

28. According to this statement,   28.____

    A. it is unnecessary to read the period at the end of a sentence
    B. typographical errors should be noted on the original copy
    C. each person should develop his own set of proofreading marks
    D. figures should be read twice

29. When questioned by his supervisor, the clerk said, "*I have never begin a new assign-*   29.____
ment until I have completely finished whatever I am working on."
This statement may BEST be characterized as

    A. *foolish;* work should be orderly
    B. *foolish;* every task must be completed sooner or later
    C. *wise;* unfinished work is an index of inefficiency
    D. *foolish;* some assignments should be undertaken immediately

30. Suppose that a clerk in your office has been transferred to another unit. After a brief   30.____
period of training, you are assigned to his duties. An important problem arises, and you
are uncertain as to the most advisable course of action.
For you to telephone the clerk whose place you are taking and to ask his advice would
be

    A. *wise;* his interest in your welfare will be stimulated
    B. *foolish;* incompetence is admitted
    C. *foolish;* learning is best accomplished by doing
    D. *wise;* useful guidance may be obtained

31. Suppose that a file cabinet, which has a capacity of 3,000 cards, now contains approxi-   31.____
mately 2,200 cards. Cards are added to the file at the average rate of 30 cards a day.
To find the number of days it will take to fill the cabinet to capacity,

    A. divide 3,000 by 30
    B. divide 2,200 by 3,000
    C. divide 800 by 30
    D. multiply 30 by the fraction 2,200 divided by 3,000

32. A *tickler file* is used CHIEFLY for   32.____

    A. unsorted papers which the file clerk has not had time to file
    B. personnel records
    C. pending matters which should receive attention at some particular time
    D. index to cross-referenced material

33. A new file clerk who has not become thoroughly familiar with the files in unable to locate   33.____
McLeod in the correspondence files under *Mo* and asks your help.
Of the following, the BEST reply to give her is that

    A. there probably is no correspondence in the files for that person
    B. she probably has the name spelled wrong and should verify the spelling
    C. she will probably find the correspondence under *McLeod* as the files are arranged
       with the prefix *Mc* considered as *Mac* (as if the name were spelled *MacLeod*)
    D. the correspondence folder for *McLeod* has evidently been misplaced or borrowed
       from the files

34. If your superior asks you a question to which you do not know the answer, you should   34.____
say

    A. "That is not my work."
    B. "I'm sorry, I do not know."
    C. "I do not know but you can look it up in the files."
    D. "Ask Miss Jones. I think she knows something about that matter."

35. Of the following, for which reason are cross-references necessary in filing?   35.____

    A. There is a choice of terms under which the correspondence may be filed.
    B. The only filing information contained in the correspondence is the name of the
       writer.
    C. Records are immediately visible without searching through the files.
    D. Persons other than file clerks can easily locate material.

36. The Federal Bureau of Investigation is a bureau in the Department of   36.____

    A. Justice   B. Defense   C. the Interior   D. State

37. A citizen of the United States who wishes to obtain a passport permitting him to visit a   37.____
foreign country should apply at the office of the United States Department of

    A. Defense   B. Justice   C. the Interior   D. State

38. The permanent headquarters of the United Nations is in   38.____

    A. Geneva   B. Moscow   C. Paris   D. New York City

39. Six gross of special drawing pencils were purchased for use in a city department.   39.____
If the pencils were used at the rate of 24 a week, the MAXIMUM number of weeks that
the six gross of pencils would last is _____ weeks.

    A. 6   B. 12   C. 24   D. 36

40. A stock clerk had 600 pads on hand. He then issued 3/8 of his supply of pads to Division   40.____
X, 1/4 to Division Y, and 1/6 to Division Z.
The number of pads remaining in stock is

    A. 48   B. 125   C. 240   D. 475

41. If a certain job can be performed by 18 clerks in 26 days, the number of clerks needed to   41.____
perform the job in 12 days is _____ clerks.

    A. 24   B. 30   C. 39   D. 52

Questions 42-50.

DIRECTIONS: Each of Questions 42 to 50 consists of four names. For each question, select the one of the four names that should be THIRD if the four names were arranged in alphabetical order in accordance with the Rules for Alphabetical Filing given below. For each question, print in the correspondingly numbered space at the right the letter preceding the name that should be THIRD in alphabetical order.

RULES FOR ALPHABETICAL FILING

NAMES OF INDIVIDUALS

(1)   *Names of individuals are to be filed in strict alphabetical order. This order is determined first according to the last name, then according to the first name or initial, and finally according to the middle name or initial (if any).*

(2)   *Where two last names are identical, the one with an initial instead of a first name precedes the one with a first name that begins with the same initial letter. For example: Cole precedes Edward Cole.*

(3)   *Where two last names are identical and the two first names are also identical, the one without a middle name or initial precedes the one with a middle name or initial. For example: Edward Cole precedes both Edward R. Cole and Edward Robert Cole.*

(4)   *Where two last names are identical and the two first names are also identical, the one with a middle initial precedes the one with a middle name beginning with the same initial letter.*
For example: Edward R. Cole precedes Edward Robert Cole.

(5)   *Prefixes such as D', De, La, Le, Mac, Mc, O', and von are considered parts of the names they precede. These names should be filed as spelled. For example: Peter La Farge precedes John Le Blanc.*

(6)   *Treat all abbreviations as if spelled out in full when the names for which they stand are commonly understood.*

NAMES OF BUSINESS ORGANIZATIONS

(1)   *Names of business organizations are filed in alphabetical order as written, except that a name containing the name of an individual is filed in accordance with the rules given for filing names of individuals. For example: John Cole Varnish Co. precedes Federal Trust Co.*

(2)   *Names composed of numerals or abbreviations are to be treated as though the numerals or abbreviations were spelled out.*

(3)   *Disregard the following in alphabetizing: and, the, of.*

SAMPLE:

(A)	Adam Dunn	(2)
(B)	E. Dunn	(3)
(C)	A. Duncan	(1)
(D)	Edward Robert Dunn	(4)

The numbers in parentheses indicate the proper alphabetical order in which these names should be filed. Since the name that should be filed THIRD is E. Dunn, the answer is B.

42. A. William Carver   B. Howard Cambell   42.____
     C. Arthur Chambers   D. Charles Banner

43. A. Paul Moore   B. William Moore   43.____
     C. Paul A. Moore   D. William Allen Moore

44. A. George Peters   B. Eric Petersen   44.____
     C. G. Peters   D. Petersen

45. A. Edward Hallam   B. Jos. Frank Hamilton   45.____
     C. Edward A. Hallam   D. Joseph F. Hamilton

46. A. Theodore Madison   B. Timothy McGill   46.____
     C. Thomas MacLane   D. Thomas A. Madison

47. A. William O'Hara   B. Arthur Gordon   47.____
     C. James DeGraff   D. Anne von Glatin

48. A. Charles Green   B. Chas. T. Greene   48.____
     C. Charles Thomas Greene   D. Wm. A. Greene

49. A. John Foss Insurance Co. B. New World Stove Co.   49.____
     C. 14th Street Dress Shop D. Arthur Stein Paper Co.

50. A. Gold Trucking Co.   B. 8th Ave. Garage   50.____
     C. The First National Bank D. The Century Novelty Co.

KEY (CORRECT ANSWERS)

1.	C	11.	A	21.	A	31.	C	41.	C
2.	D	12.	A	22.	B	32.	C	42.	A
3.	A	13.	B	23.	D	33.	C	43.	B
4.	C	14.	C	24.	A	34.	B	44.	D
5.	B	15.	C	25.	C	35.	A	45.	D
6.	C	16.	B	26.	B	36.	A	46.	D
7.	D	17.	D	27.	C	37.	D	47.	A
8.	B	18.	A	28.	D	38.	D	48.	C
9.	A	19.	C	29.	C	39.	D	49.	B
10.	B	20.	D	30.	C	40.	B	50.	C

TEST 2

DIRECTIONS: Each question or incomplete statement is followed by several suggested answers or completions. Select the one that BEST answers the question or completes the statement. *PRINT THE LETTER OF THE CORRECT ANSWER IN THE SPACE AT THE RIGHT.*

1. *The supervisor's instructions were <u>terse</u>.* The word *terse* as used in this sentence means MOST NEARLY   1.____

    A. detailed   B. harsh   C. vague   D. concise

2. *He did not wish to evade these issues.* The word *evade* as used in this sentence means MOST NEARLY   2.____

    A. avoid   B. examine   C. settle   D. discuss

3. *The prospects for an early settlement were <u>dubious</u>.* The word *dubious* as used in this sentence means MOST NEARLY   3.____

    A. strengthened   B. uncertain   C. weakened   D. cheerful

4. *The visitor was <u>morose</u>.* The word *morose* as used in this sentence means MOST NEARLY   4.____

    A. curious   B. gloomy   C. impatient   D. timid

5. *He was unwilling to <u>impede</u> the work of his unit.* The word *impede* as used in this sentence means MOST NEARLY   5.____

    A. carry out   B. criticize   C. praise   D. hinder

6. *The remuneration was unsatisfactory.* The word *remuneration* as used in this sentence means MOST NEARLY   6.____

    A. payment   B. summary   C. explanation   D. estimate

7. A *recurring* problem is one that   7.____

    A. replaces a problem that existed previously
    B. is unexpected
    C. has long been overlooked
    D. comes up from time to time

8. *His subordinates were aware of this <u>magnanimous</u> act.* The word *magnanimous* as used in this sentence means MOST NEARLY   8.____

    A. insolent   B. shrewd   C. unselfish   D. threatening

9. *The new employee is a <u>zealous</u> worker.* The word *zealous* as used in this sentence means MOST NEARLY   9.____

    A. awkward   B. untrustworthy
    C. enthusiastic   D. skillful

10. To *impair* means MOST NEARLY to   10.____

    A. weaken   B. conceal   C. improve   D. expose

11. *The unit head was in a <u>quandary</u>.* The word *quandary* as used in this sentence means MOST NEARLY   11.____

    A. violent dispute   B. puzzling predicament
    C. angry mood   D. strong position

12. *His actions were <u>judicious</u>.* The word *judicious* as used in this sentence means MOST NEARLY   12.____

    A. wise   B. biased   C. final   D. limited

13. *His report contained many <u>irrelevant</u> statements.* The word *irrelevant* as used in this sentence means MOST NEARLY   13.____

    A. unproven   B. not pertinent
    C. hard to understand   D. insincere

14. *He was not present at the <u>inception</u> of the program.* The word *inception* as used in this sentence means MOST NEARLY   14.____

    A. beginning   B. discussion   C. conclusion   D. rejection

15. The word *solicitude* means MOST NEARLY   15.____

    A. request   B. isolation   C. seriousness   D. concern

Questions 16-30.

DIRECTIONS: Each of the sentences numbered 16 to 30 may be classified MOST appropriately under one of the following four categories:
        A. faulty because of incorrect grammar or word usage
        B. faulty because of incorrect punctuation
        C. faulty because of incorrect capitalization
        D. correct

        Examine each sentence carefully. Then, in the correspondingly numbered space at the right, print the letter preceding the option which is the BEST of the four suggested above. All incorrect sentences contain but one type of error. Consider a sentence correct if it contains none of the types of errors mentioned, even though there may be other correct ways of expressing the same thought.

16. He was not informed, that he would have to work overtime.   16.____

17. The wind blew several papers off of his desk.   17.____

18. Charles Dole, who is a member of the committee, was asked to confer with commissioner Wilson.   18.____

19. Miss Bell will issue a copy to whomever asks for one.   19.____

20. Most employees, and he is no exception do not like to work overtime.   20.____

21. This is the man whom you interviewed last week. 21._____

22. Of the two cities visited, White Plains is the cleanest. 22._____

23. Although he was willing to work on other holidays, he refused to work on Labor day. 23._____

24. If an employee wishes to attend the conference, he should fill out the necessary forms. 24._____

25. The division chief reports that an engineer and an inspector is needed for this special survey. 25._____

26. The work was assigned to Miss Green and me. 26._____

27. The staff regulations state that an employee, who is frequently tardy, may receive a negative evaluation. 27._____

28. He is the kind of person who is always willing to undertake difficult assignments. 28._____

29. Mr. Wright's request cannot be granted under no conditions. 29._____

30. George Colt a new employee, was asked to deliver the report to the Domestic Relations Court. 30._____

Questions 31-40.

DIRECTIONS: Each of Questions 31 to 40 consists of four words. One of the words in each question is spelled INCORRECTLY. For each question, print in the correspondingly numbered space at the right the letter preceding the word which is INCORRECTLY spelled.

31.	A.	primery	B.	mechanic	C.	referred	D.	admissible	31._____
32.	A.	cessation	B.	beleif	C.	aggressive	D.	allowance	32._____
33.	A.	leisure	B.	authentic	C.	familiar	D.	contemptable	33._____
34.	A.	volume	B.	forty	C.	dilemma	D.	seldum	34._____
35.	A.	discrepancy	B.	aquisition	C.	exorbitant	D.	lenient	35._____
36.	A.	simultanous	B.	penetrate	C.	revision	D.	conspicuous	36._____
37.	A.	ilegible	B.	gracious	C.	profitable	D.	obedience	37._____
38.	A.	manufacturer	B.	authorize	C.	compelling	D.	pecular	38._____
39.	A.	anxious	B.	rehearsal	C.	handicaped	D.	tendency	39._____
40.	A.	meticulous	B.	accompaning	C.	initiative	D.	shelves	40._____

Questions 41-50.

DIRECTIONS: Questions 41 to 50 are based on the Personnel Record of Division X shown below. Refer to this table when answering these questions.

DIVISION X
PERSONNEL RECORD - CURRENT YEAR

EmDlovee	Bureau in Which Employed	Title	Annual Salary	No. of Days Absent		No. of Times Late
				On Vaca-tion	On Sick Leave	
Abbott	Mail Bureau	Clerk	$31,200	18	0	1
Barnes	,,	Clerk	25,200	25	3	7
Davis	,,	Typist	24,000	21	9	2
Adams	Payroll Bureau	Accountant	42,500	10	0	2
Bell	,,	Bookkeeper	31,200	23	2	5
Duke	,,	Clerk	27,600	24	4	3
Gross	,,	Clerk	21,600	12	5	7
Lane	,,	Stenographer	26,400	19	16	20
Reed	,,	Typist	22,800	15	11	11
Arnold	Record Bureau	Clerk	32,400	6	15	9
Cane	,,	Clerk	24,500	14	3	4
Fay	,,	Clerk	21,100	20	0	4
Hale	,,	Typist	25,200	18	2	7
Baker	Supply Bureau	Clerk	30,000	20	3	2
Clark	,,	Clerk	27,600	25	6	5
Ford	,,	Typist	22,800	25	4	22

41. The percentage of the total number of employees who are clerks is MOST NEARLY   41.____

   A.   25%   B.   33%   C.   38%   D.   56%

42. Of the following employees, the one who receives a monthly salary of $2,100 is   42.____

   A.   Barnes   B.   Gross   C.   Reed   D.   Clark

43. The difference between the annual salary of the highest paid clerk and that of the lowest   43.____
    paid clerk is

   A. $6,000   B. $8,400   C. $11,300   D. $20,900

44. The number of employees receiving more than $25,000 a year but less than $40,000 a   44.____
    year is

   A.   6   B.   9   C.   12   D.   15

45. The total annual salary of the employees of the Mail Bureau is   45.____

   A.   one-half of the total annual salary of the employees of the Payroll Bureau
   B.   less than the total annual salary of the employees of the Record Bureau by
        $21,600
   C.   equal to the total annual salary of the employees of the Supply Bureau
   D.   less than the total annual salary of the employees of the Payroll Bureau by $71,600

46. The average annual salary of the employees who are NOT clerks is MOST NEARLY   46.____

   A. $23,700   B. $25,450   C. $26,800   D. $27,850

47. If all the employees were given a 10% increase in pay, the annual salary of Lane would   47.____
    then be

    A. greater than that of Barnes by $1,320
    B. less than that of Bell by $4,280
    C. equal to that of Clark
    D. greater than that of Ford by $3,600

48. Of the clerks who earned less than $30,000 a year, the one who was late the FEWEST   48.____
    number of times was late _____ time(s).

    A. 1   B. 2   C. 3   D. 4

49. The bureau in which the employees were late the FEWEST number of times on an aver-   49.____
    age is the _____ Bureau.

    A. Mail   B. Payroll   C. Record   D. Supply

50. The MOST accurate of the following statements is that   50.____

    A. Reed was late more often than any other typist
    B. Bell took more time off for vacation than any other employee earning $30,000 or
       more annually
    C. of the typists, Ford was the one who was absent the fewest number of times
       because of sickness
    D. three clerks took no time off because of sickness

____

KEY (CORRECT ANSWERS)

1.	D	11.	B	21.	D	31.	A	41.	D
2.	A	12.	A	22.	A	32.	B	42.	A
3.	B	13.	B	23.	C	33.	D	43.	C
4.	B	14.	A	24.	D	34.	D	44.	B
5.	D	15.	D	25.	A	35.	B	45.	C
6.	A	16.	B	26.	D	36.	A	46.	D
7.	D	17.	A	27.	B	37.	A	47.	A
8.	C	18.	C	28.	D	38.	D	48.	C
9.	C	19.	A	29.	A	39.	C	49.	A
10.	A	20.	B	30.	B	40.	B	50.	B

EXAMINATION SECTION
TEST 1

DIRECTIONS: Each question or incomplete statement is followed by several suggested answers or completions. Select the one that BEST answers the question or completes the statement. *PRINT THE LETTER OF THE CORRECT ANSWER IN THE SPACE AT THE RIGHT.*

1. Assume that you are one of several clerks employed in the office of a city department.   1._____
Members of the public occasionally visit the office to obtain information. Because your desk is nearest the entrance to the office, most of these visitors direct their inquiries to you. One morning when every one including yourself is busy, a visitor enters the office and asks you for some readily available information.
Of the following, the BEST action for you to take is to

    A. disregard his question in the hope that he will direct his inquiry to another clerk
    B. inform him politely that you are busy now and ask him to return in the afternoon
    C. give him the requested information concisely but courteously and then continue with your work
    D. advise him to write a letter to your department so that the information can be sent to him

2. As a clerk in the payroll bureau of a city department, you have been assigned the task of   2._____
checking several payroll sheets. Your supervisor has informed you that these payroll sheets are needed by another department and must be sent to that department by 4 P.M. that day. After you have worked for a few hours, you realize that you will be unable to complete this assignment on time.
Of the following, the BEST action for you to take first is to

    A. ask a co-worker to help you
    B. check only those payroll sheets which you think are most important
    C. make sure that the payroll sheets which have been checked are sent out on time
    D. inform your supervisor of the situation

3. The switchboard operator of Department X refers a call to the department's Personnel   3._____
Bureau. Miss Jones, a clerk in the Personnel Bureau, answers this call.
Of the following ways of answering this call, the MOST acceptable one is for
Miss Jones to say

    A. "Hello."
    B. "Personnel Bureau, Miss Jones speaking."
    C. "Miss Jones speaking. To whom do you wish to speak?!'
    D. "Hello. This is Miss Jones of Department X."

4. A clerk in the mailing division of a large city department should be acquainted with the   4._____
functions of the other divisions of the department CHIEFLY because he will be

    A. able to answer questions asked by visitors regarding the department
    B. more conscientious in doing his work if he knows that other divisions of the department perform important functions
    C. in a better position to make suggestions for improving the work of the various divisions of the department
    D. able to determine the proper division to which mail is to be forwarded

5. The central filing unit of a certain city department keeps in its files records used by the various bureaus in connection with their daily work.
It is desirable for the clerks in this filing unit to refile records as soon as possible after they have been returned by the different bureaus CHIEFLY because

    5.____

    A. records which are needed can be located most easily if they have been filed
    B. such procedure develops commendable work habits among the employees
    C. records which are not filed immediately are usually filed incorrectly
    D. the accumulation of records to be filed gives the office a disorderly appearance

6. The active and inactive file material of an office is to be filed in several four-drawer filing cabinets.
Of the following, the BEST method of filing the material is, in general, to

    6.____

    A. keep inactive material in the upper drawers of the file cabinet so that such material may be easily removed for disposal
    B. keep active material in the upper drawers so that the amount of stooping by clerks using the files is reduced to a minimum
    C. assign drawers in the file cabinets alternately to active and to inactive material so that file material can be transferred easily from the active to the inactive files
    D. assign file cabinets alternately to active and to inactive material so that cross-references between the two types of material can be easily made

7. Of the following, the BEST reason for using form letters is that they

    7.____

    A. enable an individual to transmit unpleasant or disappointing communications in a gentle and sympathetic manner
    B. present the facts in a terse, business-like manner
    C. save the time of both the dictator and the typist in answering letters dealing with similar matters
    D. are flexible and can be easily changed to meet varying needs and complex situations

8. City agencies use either window envelopes or plain envelopes in mailing their correspondence, depending upon the type of mail being sent out.
When a mail clerk uses a window envelope rather than a plain envelope, he should be especially careful in

    8.____

    A. sealing and stamping the envelope
    B. affixing the correct amount of postage
    C. folding and inserting the communication
    D. checking the return address

9. As a mail clerk, you have been instructed to make sure that an important letter is received by the person to whom it is addressed.

    9.____

Of the following, the BEST action for you to take is to send the letter by
    A. registered mail   B. special delivery
    C. air mail   D. first-class mail

10. In filing, a clerk must often attach several papers together before placing them in the files.   10._____
    Usually, the MOST desirable of the following methods of attaching these papers is to

    A. pin them together
    B. staple them together
    C. attach them with a paper clip
    D. glue them together

11. It is a common practice in answering a letter of inquiry to make a copy of the reply.   11._____
    A clerk should know that, of the following, the BEST procedure to follow with the copy
    is to

    A. file it with the letter it answers
    B. file it alphabetically in a separate copy file
    C. file it chronologically in a separate copy file and destroy the copy after thirty days
    D. enclose it with the letter of reply

12. Suppose that much of the work of your office involves computation of statistical data.   12._____
    This computation is being done without the use of adding machines. You believe the
    work could be done more efficiently if adding machines were used.
    Of the following, the BEST action for you to take is to

    A. carry out your assignments without comment, since it is not your function to
       recommend revisions in office practices
    B. have other clerks who agree with you sign a memorandum requesting your
       supervisor to install adding machines
    C. obtain concrete facts to support your views and then take this matter up with
       your supervisor
    D. point out to your supervisor every time an error is made that it would not have
       occurred if adding machines had been used

13. A clerk employed in the central file section of a city department has been requested to   13._____
    obtain a certain card which is kept in an alphabetic file containing several thousand cards.
    The clerk finds that this card is not in its proper place and that there is no out card to aid
    him in tracing its location.
    Of the following, the course of action which would be LEAST helpful to him in locating the
    missing card would be for him to

    A. secure the assistance of his superior
    B. look at several cards filed immediately before and after the place where the
       missing card should be filed
    C. ask the other clerks in the file section whether they have this card
    D. prepare an out card and place it where the missing card should be filed

14. The one of the following types of computer software which requires the use of   14._____
    spreadsheets is

    A. Excel   B. Acrobat   C. Outlook   D. Safari

15. A clerk assigned to file correspondence in a subject file would be MOST concerned with   15._____
    the
    A. name of the sender   B. main topic of the correspondence
    C. city and state of the sender   D. date of the correspondence

16. Assume that you are responsible for storing and distributing supplies in a city department.   16.____
The one of the following factors which you should consider LEAST important in selecting a
suitable place in the stock room for storing a particular item is

    A. the frequency of requests for it
    B. its perishability
    C. its size
    D. the importance of the bureaus using it

17. A clerk in charge of the supply room of a city department notices that one of the bureaus   17.____
is asking for considerably more stationery than it has requested in the past.
For him to inquire into the reasons for the increased demand would be

    A. *desirable*; the amount of stationery used by a bureau should remain constant
    B. *undesirable*; the increased demand may be due to waste, a condition beyond his control
    C. *desirable*; he will be better able to estimate future needs for stationery
    D. *undesirable*; he may be accused of meddling in matters which do not concern him

18. One of the first things an executive usually looks for when he arrives in the morning is   18.____
his mail.
Of the following, the MOST valid implication on the basis of this statement is that

    A. letters addressed to an executive should be answered in the order in which
       they are received
    B. whenever possible, mail for an executive should be on his desk before his
       arrival in the morning
    C. letters to a city department should be addressed to the department head
    D. the first task of an executive upon his arrival in the morning should be to
       answer his mail

19. Persons in the employ of a public agency generally come into contact with many people   19.____
outside of working hours. In these contacts, the government employee represents to the
public the quality, competence, and stature of public employees as a group.
The one of the following statements which is the MOST valid implication of the above
observation is that

    A. the responsibilities of a public employee cease after office hours
    B. government employees who come into contact with the public during working hours
       should be more efficient than those who have no contact with the public
    C. a public employee, by his behavior during social activities, can raise the prestige of
       public employment
    D. employees of a private company have greater responsibilities during office hours
       than employees of a public agency

20. Filing, in a way, is a form of recording.   20.____

The one of the following which BEST explains this statement is that
    A. no other records are required if a proper filing system is used
    B. important records should, as a rule, be kept in filing cabinets
    C. a good system of record keeping eliminates the necessity for a filing system
    D. filing a letter or document is, in effect, equivalent to making a record of its contents

21. In standardizing clerical tasks, one should attempt to eliminate the undesirable elements   21._____
and to retain the desirable ones.
Of the following, the MOST valid implication of the above statement is that

    A. a task containing undesirable elements cannot be standardized
    B. standardized clerical tasks should not contain any unnecessary steps
    C. interesting clerical tasks are easier to standardize than monotonous clerical tasks
    D. a clerical task cannot have both desirable and undesirable elements

22. The efficiency of office workers in affected by the quality of the services provided to   22._____
facilitate their work.
The one of the following statements which is the BEST illustration of the above judgment
is that

    A. a poorly run mail room will hamper the work of the office staff
    B. continual tardiness on the part of an office worker will be reflected in the erformance of his work
    C. a system of promoting office workers through competitive examinations will increase their efficiency
    D. the use of a time clock will improve the quality of the work performed

23. In elections held in various states, the provisions relating to veterans' preference have   23._____
been amended to conform with Federal practice.
In general, the MOST accurate statement regarding veterans' preference in civil service
open competitive examinations for original appointment is that

    A. disabled veterans passing an examination will be given 10 additional points and non-disabled veterans passing an examination will be given 5 additional points
    B. disabled veterans passing an examination will be placed on top of the eligible list; non-disabled veterans will be placed after them; and non-veterans will be placed last on the list
    C. only disabled veterans will be given 5 additional points; no additional points will be given to nondisabled veterans
    D. the granting of additional points to all disabled and non-disabled veterans will be discontinued

24. Suppose that you are assigned to the information desk in your department. Your function   24._____
is to give information to members of the public who telephone or call in person. It is a busy
period of the year. There is a line of seventeen people waiting to speak to you. Because you
are constantly being interrupted by telephone calls for information, however, you are unable
to give any attention to the people waiting on line. The line is increasing in length.
Of the following, the BEST action for you to take is to

    A. explain courteously to the people on line that you will probably be unable to help them
    B. advise the people at the end of the line that you will probably not reach them for some time and suggest that they come back when you are less busy
    C. ask the switchboard operator to answer telephone requests for information herself instead of putting the calls on your extension
    D. ask your supervisor to assign another clerk to answer telephone calls so that you can give your full attention to the people on line

25. Suppose that you are acting as the receptionist in your department. A man comes up to you, introduces himself as Mr. Smith, and says that he has an appointment with Mr. Brown, one of the clerks in your department. You know that Mr. Brown has been called out of the office for a few days on important business. Upon learning of Mr. Brown's absence, Mr. Smith asks whether someone else can help him. For you to telephone Mr. Brown's office and ask whether some other clerk there can help Mr. Smith would be WISE mainly because   25.___

    A. Mr. Smith's business is probably confidential
    B. another clerk has probably been assigned to do Mr. Brown's work in Mr. Brown's absence
    C. Mr. Brown may return unexpectedly
    D. it is uncertain whether Mr. Smith actually does have an appointment with Mr. Brown

26. One of your duties may be to deliver copies of administrative orders to administrators in your department. It is not necessary for an administrator to sign a receipt for his copy of an order. One of the administrators to whom you are requested to deliver a copy of an order is not at his desk when you make your usual tour of the office. Of the following, the BEST action for you to take is to   26.___

    A. keep this order until a later order is issued and then deliver both orders at the same time
    B. wait until you meet the administrator in the corridor and give him his copy in person
    C. leave a note on the administrator's desk requesting him to call
    D. leave the administrator's copy of the order on his desk

27. One of your duties may be to deliver inter-office mail to all of the offices in the department in which you work.
Of the following, the BEST procedure for you to follow before you deliver the letters is, in general, to arrange them on the basis of the   27.___

    A. offices to which the letters are to be delivered
    B. dates on which the letters were written
    C. specific persons by whom the letters were signed
    D. offices from which the letters come

28. The population census of the country is undertaken every ten years by the United States Department of   28.___
    A. Labor   B. the Treasury   C. Commerce   D. the Interior

29. Of the following pairs of offices in the Federal government, the pair which is held by the same individual is   29.___
    A. Secretary of Defense and Secretary of the Army
    B. Chairman of the Atomic Energy Commission and Chairman of the Tennessee Valley Authority
    C. Chief Justice of the United States Supreme Court and Attorney General
    D. Vice President of the United States and President of the Senate

30. A clerk who is familiar with the organization and activities of the United Nations should know, of the following statements, the MOST accurate one is that   30.___
    A. the permanent headquarters of the United Nations is in Geneva, Switzerland
    B. devaluation of the currency of a member nation must be approved by the United Nations General Assembly
    C. there are five permanent members on the United Nations Security Council
    D. the Economic Cooperation Administration (ECA) is under the jurisdiction of the United Nations Secretary General

31. In anticipation of a seasonal increase in the amount of work to be performed by his   31._____
   division, a division chief prepared the following list of additional temporary employees
   needed by his division and the amount of time they would be employed:
      26 cashiers, each at $24,000 a year, for 2 months
      15 laborers, each at $85.00 a day, for 50 days
       6 clerks, each at $21,000 a year, for 3 months
   The total approximate cost for this additional personnel would be MOST NEARLY

       A. $200,000   B. $250,000   C. $500,000   D. $600,000

32. A calculating machine company offered to sell a city agency 4 calculating machines at a   32._____
   discount of 15% from the list price, and to allow the agency $85 for each of its two old
   machines. The list price of the new machines is $625 per machine.
   If the city agency accepts this offer, the amount of money it will have to provide for the
   purchase of these four machines is

       A. $1,785   B. $2,295   C. $1,955   D. $1,836

33. A stationery buyer was offered bond paper at the following price scale: 33._____
   $2.86 per ream for the first 1,000 reams
   $2.60 per ream for the next 4,000 reams
   $2.40 per ream for each additional ream beyond 5,000 reams
   If the buyer ordered 10,000 reams of paper, the average cost per ream, computed to the
   NEAREST cent, was

       A. $2.48   B. $2.53   C. $2.62   D. $2.72

34. A clerk has 5.70% of his salary deducted for his retirement pension.   34._____
   If this clerk's annual salary is $20,400, the monthly deduction for his retirement pension is

       A. $298.20   B. $357.90   C. $1,162.80   D. $96.90

35. In a certain bureau, two-thirds of the employees are clerks and the remainder is typists.   35._____
   If there are 90 clerks, then the number of typists in this bureau is

       A. 135   B. 45   C. 120   D. 30

Questions 36-45.

DIRECTIONS: Assume that the code tables shown below are used by a city department in
           classifying its employees. Questions 36 to 45 are to be answered on the basis
           of these tables. In accordance with these code tables, each employee in the
           department is assigned a code number consisting of ten digits arranged from
           left to right in the following order:
              I.   Division in which Employed
              II.   Title of Position
              III. Annual Salary
              IV.   Age
              V.   Number of Years Employed in Department

           Example: A clerk is 21 years old, has been employed in the department for three
           years, and is working in the Supply Division at a yearly salary of $25,000. His code
           number should be 90-115-13-02-2.

Questions 36-45.

DIRECTIONS: Assume that the code tables shown below are used by a city department in classifying its employees. Questions 36 to 45 are to be answered on the basis of these tables. In accordance with these code tables, each employee in the department is assigned a code number consisting of ten digits arranged from left to right in the following order:

VI.   Division in which Employed
VII.   Title of Position
VIII.   Annual Salary
IX.   Age
X.   Number of Years Employed in Department

Example: A clerk is 21 years old, has been employed in the department for three years, and is working in the Supply Division at a yearly salary of $25,000. His code number should be 90-115-13-02-2.

DEPARTMENTAL CODE

TABLE I		TABLE II		TABLE III		TABLE IV		TABLE V	
Code No.	Division in Which Employed	Code No.	Title of position	Code No.	Annual Salary	Code No.	Age	Code No.	No. of years Employed in Dept.
10-	Accounting Division	115-	Clek	11-	$18,000 or less	01-	under 20 yrs	1-	less than 1 yrs
20-	Construction Division	155-	Typist	12-	$18,001 to $24,000	02-	20 to 29 yrs	2-	1 to 5 yrs
30-	Engineering Division	175-	Steno- grapher	13-	$24,001 to $30,000	03-	30 to 39 yrs	3-	6 to 10 yrs
40-	Information Division	237-	Book- Keeper	14-	$30,001 to $36,000	04-	40 to 49 yrs	4-	11 to 15 yrs
50-	Maintenance Division	345-	Statis- tician	15-	$36,001 to $45,000	05-	50 to 59 yrs	5-	16 to 25 yrs
60-	Personnel Division	545-	Store- Keeper	16-	$45,001 to $60,000	06-	62 to 69 yrs	6-	26 to 35 yrs
70-	Record Division	633-	Drafts- Man	17-	$60,001 to $70,000	07- over	70 yrs or over	7-	36 yrs. or over
80-	Research Division	665-	Civil- Engineer	18-	$70,001 or over				
90-	Supply Division	865-	Machinist						
		915-	Porter						

36. A draftsman employed in the Engineering Division yearly salary of $34,800 is 36 years old and has employed in the department for 9 years.
He should be coded

    A. 20-633-13-04-3   B. 50-665-14-04-4
    C. 30-865-13-03-4   D. 30-633-14-03-3

36._____

37. A porter employed in the Maintenance Division at a yearly salary of $28,800 is 52 years old and has been employed in the department for 6 years.
He should be coded

    A. 50-915-12-03-3   B. 90-545-12-05-3
    C. 50-915-13-05-3   D. 90-545-13-03-3

37._____

38. Richard White, who has been employed in the department for 12 years, receives $50,000 a year as a civil engineer in the Construction Division. He is 38 years old.
He should be coded
    A. 20-665-16-03-4   B. 20-665-15-02-1
    C. 20-633-14-04-2   D. 20-865-15-02-5

38._____

39. An 18-year-old clerk appointed to the department six months ago is assigned to the Record Division. His annual salary is $21,600.
He should be coded

    A. 70-115-11-01-1   B. 70-115-12-01-1
    C. 70-115-12-02-1   D. 70-155-12-01-1

39._____

40. An employee has been coded 40-155-12-03-3.
Of the following statements made regarding this employee, the MOST accurate one is that he is

    A. a clerk who has been employed in the department for at least 6 years
    B. a typist who receives an annual salary which does not exceed $24,000
    C. under 30 years of age and has been employed in the department for at least
        11 years
    D. employed in the Supply Division at a salary which exceeds $18,000 per annum

40._____

41. Of the following statements regarding an employee who is coded 60-175-13-01-2, the LEAST accurate statement is that this employee
    A. is a stenographer in the Personnel Division
    B. has been employed in the department for at least one year
    C. receives an annual salary which exceeds $24,000
    D. is more than 20 years of age

41._____

42. The following are the names of our employees of the department with their code numbers:

42._____

James Black, 80-345-15-03-4;
William White, 30-633-14-03-4;
Sam Green, 80-115-12-02-3;
John Jones, 10-237-13-04-5.

If a salary increase is to be given to the employees who have been employed in the department for 11 years or more and who earn less than $36,001 a year, the two of the above employees who will receive a salary increase are

   A. John Jones and William White
   B. James Black and Sam Green
   C. James Black and William White
   D. John Jones and Sam Green

43. Code number 50-865-14-02-6, which has been assigned to a machinist, contains an obvious inconsistency. This inconsistency involves the figures   43._____

   A. 50-865   B. 865-14   C. 14-02   D. 02-6

44. Ten employees were awarded merit prizes for outstanding service during the year.   44._____
   Their code numbers were:

   80-345-14-04-4   40-155-12-02-2
   40-155-12-04-4   10-115-12-02-2
   10-115-13-03-2   80-115-13-02-2
   80-175-13-05-5   10-115-13-02-3
   10-115-12-04-3   30-633-14-04-4

   Of these ten outstanding employees, the number who were clerks employed in the Accounting Division at a salary ranging from $24,001 to $30,000 per annum is

   A. 1   B. 2   C. 3   D. 4

45. The MOST accurate of the following statements regarding the ten outstanding employees   45._____
   listed in Question 44 above is that

   A. fewer than half of the employees were under 40 years of age
   B. there were fewer typists than stenographers
   C. four of the employees were employed in the department 11 years or more
   D. two of the employees in the Research Division receive annual salaries ranging from $30,001 to $36,000

Questions 46-55.

DIRECTIONS: Questions 46 to 55 consist of groups of names. For each group, three different filing arrangements of the names in the group are given. In only one of these arrangements are the names in correct filing order according to the alphabetic filing rules which are given below. For each group, select the one arrangement, lettered A, B, or C, which is CORRECT and indicate in the space at the right the letter which corresponds to the CORRECT arrangement of names.

RULES FOR ALPHABETIC FILING

NAMES OF INDIVIDUALS

   (1) The names of individuals are to be filed in strict alphabetic order. The order of filing is: first according to the last name; then according to the first name or initial; and finally according to the middle name or initial.

(2) *Where two last names are identical, the one with an initial instead of the first name precedes the one with a first name beginning with the same initial letter. For example: D. Smith and D.J. Smith precede Donald Smith.*

(3) *Where two individuals with identical last names also have identical first names or initials, the one without a middle name or initial precedes the one with a middle name or initial. For example: D. Smith precedes D.J. Smith, and Donald Smith precedes Donald J. Smith.*

(4) *Where two individuals with identical last names also have identical first names or initials, the one with an initial instead of the middle name precedes the one with a middle name beginning with the same initial letter. For example: Donald J. Smith precedes Donald Joseph Smith.*

NAMES OF BUSINESS ORGANIZATIONS

The names of business organizations are to be filed in alphabetic order as written, except that the names of an organization containing the name of an individual is filed alphabetically according to the name of the individual as described in the above rules. For example: John Burke Wine Co. precedes Central Storage Corp.

ADDITIONAL RULES

(1) *Names composed of numerals or of abbreviations of names are to be treated as if the numerals or the abbreviations were spelled out.*
(2) *Prefixes such as De, Di, O', Le, and La are considered as part of the names they precede.*
(3) *Names beginning with "Mc" and "Mac" are to be filed as spelled.*
(4) *The following titles and designations are to be disregarded in filing: Dr., Mr., Jr., Sr., D.D.S., and M.D.*
(5) *The following are to be disregarded when they occur in the names of business organizations: the, of, and.*

SAMPLE ITEM:

ARRANGEMENT A	ARRANGEMENT B	ARRANGEMENT C
Robert Morse	R. Moss	R. T. Morse
Ralph Nixon	R. T. Morse	Robert Morse
R. T. Morse	Ralph Nixon	R. Moss
R. Moss	Robert Morse	Ralph Nixon

The CORRECT arrangement is C; the answer should, therefore, be C

46.
ARRANGMENT A	ARRANGEMENT B	ARRANGEMENT C	46.____
R. B. Stevens	Aled T. Stevens	R.Stevens	
Chas. Stevennson	R. B. Stevens	Robert Stevens, Sr.	
Robert Stevensm, Sr.	Robert Stevens, Sr.	Alfred T. Steven s	
Alfred T. Stevens	Chas. Stevenson	Chas. Stevenson	

47.
ARRANGEMENT A	ARRANGEMENT B	ARRANGEMENT C	47.____
Mr. A. T. Breen	John Brewington	Dr. Otis C. Breen	
Dr. Otis C. Breen	Amelia K. Brewington	Mr. A. T. Breen	
Amelia K Brewington	Dr. Otis C. Breen	John Brewington	
John Brewington	Mr. A. T. Breen	Amelia K. Brewington	

48.   ARRANGEMENT A   ARRANGEMENT B   ARRANGEMENT C   48._____

ARRANGEMENT A	ARRANGEMENT B	ARRANGEMENT C
J. Murphy	John Murphy	J. Murphy
J. J. Murphy	John J. Murphy	John Murphy
John Murphy	J. Murphy	J. J. Murphy
John J. Murphy	J. J. Murphy	John J. Murphy

49.   ARRANGEMENT A   ARRANGEMENT B   ARRANGEMENT C   49._____

ARRANGEMENT A	ARRANGEMENT B	ARRANGEMENT C
Anthoney Dibuono	Geo. T. Burns, Jr.	George Burns, Sr.
George Burns, Sr	George Burns, Sr.	George T. Burns, Jr.
Geo. T. Burns, Jr.	Anthony DiBuono	Alan J. Byrnes
Alan J. Byrnes	Alan J. Byrnes	Anthony DiBuono

50.   ARRANGEMENT A   ARRANGEMENT B   ARRANGEMENT C   50._____

ARRANGEMENT A	ARRANGEMENT B	ARRANGEMENT C
James Macauley	James Macauley	Bernard J. Macmahon
Frank A. Mclowery	Francis Macloughry	Francis MacLaughry
Francis Maclaughry	Bernard J.Macmahon	Frank A. McLowery
Bernard J. MacMahon	Frank A. McLowery	James Macauley

51.   ARRANGEMENT A   ARRANGEMENT B   ARRANGEMENT C   51._____

ARRANGEMENT A	ARRANGEMENT B	ARRANGEMENT C
A. J. DiBartolo, Sr.	J. A. Bartolo	Anthony J. Bartolo
A. P.DiBartolo	Anthony J. Bartolo	J. A. Bartolo
J. A. Bartolo	A. J. DiBartolo	A. J. DiBartolo, Sr
Anthony J. Bartolo	A. J. DiBartolo, Sr.	A. P. DiBartolo

52.   ARRANGEMENT A   ARRANGEMENT B   ARRANGEMENT C   52._____

ARRANGEMENT A	ARRANGEMENT B	ARRANGEMENT C
Edward Holmes Corp.	Edward Holmes Corp.	Hillside Trust Corp.
Hillside Trust Corp.	Hillside Trust Corp.	Edward Holmes Corp
Standard Insurance Co.	The Industrial Surety Co.	The Industrial Surety Co.
The Industrial Surety Co	Standard Insurance Co.	Standard Insurance Co.

53.   ARRANGEMENT A   ARRANGEMENT B   53._____

ARRANGEMENT A	ARRANGEMENT B
Cooperative Credit Co.	Chas, Cooke Chemical Corp.
Chas. Cooke Chemical Corp.	Cooperative Credit Co.
John Fuller Baking Co.	4th Avenue Express Co.
4th Avenue Express Co.	John Fuller Baking Co.

     ARRANGEMENT C

4th Avenue Express Co.
John Fuller Baking Co.
Chas. Cooke Chemical Corp.
Cooperative Credit Co.

54.   ARRANGEMENT A   ARRANGEMENT B   ARRANGEMENT C   54._____

ARRANGEMENT A	ARRANGEMENT B	ARRANGEMENT C
Mr. R. McDaniels	F. L. Ramsey	Robert darling, Jr.
Robert Darling, Jr.	Mr. R. McDaniels	Charles DeRhone
F. L. Ramsey	Charles DeRhone	Mr. R. Mcdaniels
Charles DeRhone	Robert Darling, Jr.	F. L. Ramsey

55.

ARRANGEMENT A	ARRANGEMENT B	ARRANGEMENT C 55._____
New York Ominibus Corp.	John J. O'Brien Co.	Nova Scotia Canning Co.
New York Shipping Co.	New York Ominibus Ciorp.	John J. O'Brien Co.
Nove Scotia Canning Co.	New York Shipping Co.	New York Ominibus Corp.
John J. O'Brien Co.	Nove Scotia Canning Co.	New York shipping Co.

56. He was asked to *pacify* the visitor. The word pacify means MOST NEARLY   56._____

    A. escort   B. interview   C. calm   D. detain

57. To say that a certain document is *authentic* means MOST NEARLY that it is   57._____

    A. fictitious   B. well written   C. priceless   D. genuine

58. A clerk who is *meticulous* in performing his work is one who is   58._____

    A. alert to improved techniques
    B. likely to be erratic and unpredictable
    C. excessively careful of small details
    D. slovenly and inaccurate

59 A pamphlet which is *replete* with charts and graphs is one which   59._____

    A. deals with the construction of charts and graphs
    B. is full of charts and graphs
    C. substitutes illustrations for tabulated data
    D. is in need of charts and graphs

60. His former secretary was *diligent* in carrying out her duties. The word diligent means   60._____
MOST NEARLY

    A. incompetent   B. cheerful   C. careless   D. industrious

61. To *supepsede* means MOST NEARLY to   61._____

    A. take the place of   B. come before
    C. be in charge of   D. divide into equal parts

62. He sent the *irate* employee to the pepsonnel manager. The word *irate* means   62._____
MOST NEARLY

    A. irresponsible   B. untidy   C. insubordinate   D. angry

63. An *ambiguous* statement is one which is   63._____
    A forceful and convincing
    B capable of being understood in more than one sense
    C based upon good judgment and sound reasoning processes
    D uninteresting and too lengthy

64. To *extol* means MOST NEARLY to   64.____

    A. summon   B. praise   C. reject   D. withdraw

65. The word *proximity* means MOST NEARLY 65.____

   A. similarity B. exactness C. harmony D. nearness

66. His friends had a *detrimental* influence on him. The word detrimental means 66.____
   MOST NEARLY

   A. favorable B. lasting C. harmful D. short-lived

67. The chief inspector relied upon the *veracity* of his inspectors. The word veracity means 67.____
   MOST NEARLY
   A. speed B. assistance C. shrewdness D. truthfulness

68. There was much *diversity* in the suggestions submitted. The word diversity means 68.____
   MOST NEARLY

   A. similarity B. value C. triviality D. variety

69. The survey was concerned with the problem of *indigence.* The word indigence means 69.____
   MOST NEARLY

   A. poverty B. corruption C. intolerance D. morale

70. The investigator considered this evidence to be *extraneous.* The word extraneous 70.____
   means MOST NEARLY

   A. significant   B. pertinent but unobtainable
   C. not essential   D. inadequate

71. He was surppised at the *temerity* of the new employee. The word temerity means 71.____
   MOST NEARLY

   A. shyness B. enthusiasm C. rashness D. self-control

72. The term *ex officio* means MOST NEARLY 72.____

   A. expelled from office
   B. a former holder of a high office
   C. without official approval
   D. by virtue of office or position

Questions 73-82.

DIRECTIONS: Questions 73 to 82 consist of four words each. One word in each row is
   INCORRECTLY spelled. For each item, print in the correspondingly numbered
   space at the right the letter preceding the word which is INCORRECTLY spelled.

73.	A. apparent	B. superintendent	C. releive	D. calendar	73.____
74.	A. foreign	B. negotiate	C. typical	D. discipline	74.____
75.	A. posponed	B. argument	C. susceptible	D. deficit	75.____
76.	A. preferred	B. column	C. peculiar	D. equiped	76.____

77.	A. exaggerate	B. disatisfied	C. repetition	D. already	77 _____
78.	A. livelihood	B. physician	C. obsticle	D. strategy	78._____
79.	A. courageous	B. ommission	C. ridiculous	D. awkward	79._____
80.	A. sincerely	B. abundance	C. negligable	D. elementary	80._____
81.	A. obsolete	B. mischievous	C. enumerate	D. atheletic	81._____
82.	A. fiscel	B. beneficiary	C. concede	D. translate	82._____

Questions 83-97

DIRECTIONS: Each of the following sentences may be classified MOST appropriately under one of the following four categories:
   A. faulty because of incorrect grammar
   B. faulty because of incorrect punctuation
   C. faulty because of incorrect capitalization
   D. correct
Examine each sentence carefully. Then, in the correspondingly numbered space at the right, print the letter preceding the option which is the BEST of the four suggested above. All incorrect sentences contain but one type of error. Consider a sentence correct if it contains none of the types of errors mentioned, even though there may be other eorrect ways of expressing the same thought.

83. Neither of the two administrators are going to attend the conference being held in Washington, D.C.   83._____

84. Since Miss Smith and Miss Jones have more experience than us, they have been given more responsible duties.   84._____

85. Mr. Shaw the supervisor of the stock room maintains an inventory of stationery and office supplies.   85._____

86. Inasmuch as this matter affects both you and I, we should take joint action.   86._____

87. Who do you think will be able to perform this highly technical work?   87._____

88. Of the two employees, John is considered the most competent.   88._____

89. He is not coming home on tuesday; we expect him next week.   89._____

90. Stenographers, as well as typists must be able to type rapidly and accurately.   90._____

91. Having been placed in the safe we were sure that the money would not be stolen   91._____

92. Only the employees who worked overtime last week may leave one hour earlier today.   92._____

93. We need someone who can speak french fluently.   93._____

94. A tall, elderly, man entered the office and asked to see Mr. Brown.   94._____

95. The clerk insisted that he had filed the correspondence in the proper cabinet.   95._____

96. "Will you assist us," he asked?   96.____

97. According to the information contained in the report, a large quantity of paper and envelopes were used by this bureau last year.   97.__

Questions 98-100.

DIRECTIONS: Items 98 to 100 are a test of your proofreading ability.
Each item consists of Copy I and Copy II. You are to assume that Copy I in each item is correct. Copy II, which is meant to be a duplicate of Copy I, may contain some typographical errors.. In each item, compare Copy II with Copy I and determine the number of errors in Copy II. If there are:
         no errors, mark your answer A;
         1 or 2 errors, mark your answer B;
         3 or 4 errors, mark your answer C;
         5 or 6 errors, mark your answer D;
         7 errors or more, mark your answer E.

98. COPY I   98.__

The Commissioner, before issuing any such license, shall cause an investigation to be made of the premises named and described in such application, to determine whether all the provisions of the sanitary code, building code, state industrial code, state minimum wage law, local laws, regulations of municipal agencies, and other requirements of this article are fully observed. (Section B32-169.0 of Article 23.)

COPY II

The Commissioner, before issuing any such license shall cause an investigation to be made of the premises named and described tn such appleCation, to determine whether all the provisions of the sanitary code, bilding code, state tndustrial code, state minimum wage laws, local laws, regulations of municipal agencies, and other requirements of this article are fully observed. (Section E32-169.0 of Article 23.)

99. COPY I   99.__

Among the persons who have been appointed to various agencies are John Queen, 9 West 55th Street, Brooklyn; Joseph Blount, 2497 Durward Road, Bronx; Lawrence K. Eberhardt, 3194 Bedford Street, Manhattan; Reginald L. Darcy, 1476 Allerton Drive, Bronx; and Benjamin Ledwith, 177 Greene Street, Manhattan.

COPY II

Among the persons who have been appointed to various agencies are John Queen, 9 West 56th Street,Brooklyn, Joseph Blount, 2497 Dureward Road, Bronx; Lawrence K. Eberhart, 3194 Belford Street, Manhattan; Reginald L. Darcey, 1476 Allerton drive, Bronx; and Benjamin Ledwith, 177 Green Street, Manhattan.

100. COPY I   100.__

Except as hereinafter provided, it shall be unlawful to use, store or have on hand any inflammable motion picture film in quantities greater than one standard or two sub-standard reels, or aggregating more than two thousand feet in length, or more than ten pounds in weight without the permit required by this section.

COPY II

Except as herinafter provided, it shall be unlawfull to use, store or have on hand any inflammable motion picture film, in quantities greater than one standard or two substandard reels or aggregating more than two thousand feet in length, or more than ten pounds in weight without the permit required by this section.

KEY (CORRECT ANSWERS)

1.	C	26.	D	51.	C	76.	D
2.	D	27.	A	52.	C	77.	B
3.	B	28.	C	53.	B	78.	C
4.	D	29.	D	54.	C	79.	B
5.	A	30.	C	55.	A	80.	C
6.	B	31.	A	56.	C	81.	D
7.	C	32.	C	57.	D	82.	A
8.	C	33.	B	58.	C	83.	A
9.	A	34.	D	59.	B	84.	A
10.	B	35.	B	60.	D	85.	B
11.	A	36.	B	61.	A	86.	A
12.	C	37.	C	62.	D	87.	D
13.	D	38.	A	63.	B	88.	A
14.	A	39.	B	64.	B	89.	C
15.	B	40.	B	65.	D	90.	B
16.	D	41.	D	66.	C	91.	A
17.	C	42.	A	67.	D	92.	D
18.	B	43.	D	68.	D	93.	C
19.	C	44.	B	69.	A	94.	B
20.	D	45.	C	70.	C	95.	D
21.	B	46.	B	71.	C	96.	B
22.	A	47.	A	72.	D	97.	A
23.	A	48.	A	73.	C	98.	D
24.	D	49.	C	74.	D	99.	E
25.	B	50.	B	75.	A	100.	E

EXAMINATION SECTION
TEST 1

DIRECTIONS: Each question or incomplete statement is followed by several suggested answers or completions. Select the one that BEST answers the question or completes the statement. *PRINT THE LETTER OF THE CORRECT ANSWER IN THE SPACE AT THE RIGHT.*

1. Assume that you have been assigned by your supervisor to file some record cards in a cabinet. All the cards in this cabinet are supposed to be kept in strict alphabetical order. You know that important work is being held up because certain cards in this cabinet cannot be located. While filing the records given you, you come across a card which is not in its correct alphabetical place.
   Of the following, the BEST reason for you to bring this record to the attention of your supervisor is that

   A. errors in filing are more serious than other types of errors
   B. your alertness in locating the card should be rewarded
   C. the filing system may be at fault, rather than the employee who misfiled the card
   D. time may be saved by such action

1.____

2. Assume that you are the receptionist for Mr. Brown, an official in your department. It is your duty to permit only persons having important business to see this official; otherwise, you are to refer them to other members of the staff. A man tells you that he must see Mr. Brown on a very urgent and confidential matter. He gives you his name and says that Mr. Brown knows him, but he does not wish to tell you the nature of the matter.
   Of the following, the BEST action for you to take under these circumstances is to

   A. permit this man to see Mr. Brown without further question since the matter seems to be urgent
   B. refer this man to another member of the staff, since Mr. Brown may not wish to see him
   C. call Mr. Brown and explain the situation to him, and ask him whether he wishes to see this man
   D. tell this man that you will permit him to see Mr. Brown only if he informs you of the nature of his business

2.____

3. You are given copies of an important official notice, together with a memorandum stating that each of the employees listed on the memorandum is to receive a copy of the official notice.
   In order to have definite proof that each of the employees listed has received a copy of the notice, the BEST of the following courses of action for you to take as you hand the notice to each of the employees is to

   A. put your initial next to the employee's name on the memorandum
   B. ask the employee to sign the notice you have given in your presence
   C. have the employee put his signature next to his name on the memorandum
   D. ask the employee to read the notice in your presence

3.____

4. Suppose that you are assigned to the information window of a city department where you come in daily contact with many people. On one occasion, a man asks you for some information in a very arrogant and rude manner.
Of the following, the BEST reason for you to give this man the requested information politely is that

    A. he may not mean to be rude; it may just be his manner of speech
    B. it is the duty of city employees to teach members of the public to be polite
    C. he will probably apologize for his manner when he sees that you are polite
    D. city employees are expected to be courteous to the public

4._____

5. Assume that you have been placed in charge of a stock room in a city department and that one of your duties is to take a periodic inventory of the supplies you have on hand.
Of the following, the BEST justification for this procedure is

    A. you will know which supplies are running low
    B. accurate records need not be kept in all stock rooms
    C. you will become more familiar with the location of the different items in the stock room
    D. it will prevent the needless waste of supplies by the employees of the department

5._____

6. It is an accepted practice to have the initials of the person who dictates a letter, as well as those of the person who types it, appear in the lower left-hand corner of the letter.
Of the following, the CHIEF justification for this procedure is that it

    A. may be used as a means of measuring output of work
    B. fixes responsibility
    C. aids in filing
    D. avoids the need for making carbon copies

6._____

7. Suppose that you are given several sheets containing an unalphabetized list of 500 names and a corresponding set of 500 disarranged cards. Your supervisor asks you to check to see that for every name on the list there is a corresponding card.
Of the following, the MOST efficient procedure for you to follow is to

    A. arrange both the cards and the names on the list in alphabetical order and check one against the other
    B. alphabetize the list only and check each card in turn against the names on the list
    C. alphabetize the cards only and check each name on the list in turn against the cards
    D. alphabetize neither the cards nor the list, but take each card in turn and find the corresponding name on the list

7._____

8. The clerk could not recall the name of the person to whom his supervisor had requested him to make a check payable. He therefore made it payable to *Cash*.
This action on the part of the clerk is

    A. to be praised; he showed ingenuity
    B. to be criticized; if lost, the check might be cashed by anyone finding it
    C. inexcusable; a check must be made payable to a definite person
    D. correct; in the future, he should make all checks payable to *Cash*

8._____

9. Assume that one of your duties as a clerk is to keep a constantly changing mailing list up-to-date.
Of the following, the BEST method for you to follow is to use use a(n)

    A.   alphabetical card index with loose cards, one for each name
    B.   bound volume with a separate page or group of pages for each letter
    C.   loose-leaf notebook with names beginning with the same letter listed on the same sheet or group of sheets
    D.   typed list, add names at end of the list, and retype periodically in proper alphabetical order

9.____

10. In evaluating the effectiveness of a filing system, the one of the following criteria which you should consider MOST important is the

    A.   safety of material in the event of a fire
    B.   ease with which material may be located
    C.   quantity of papers which can be filed
    D.   extent to which material in the filing system is being used

10.____

11. A set of cards numbered from 1 to 300 has been filed in numerical order in such a way that the highest number is at the front of the file and the lowest number is at the rear. It is desired that the cards be reversed to run in ascending order.
The BEST of the following methods that can be used in performing this task is to begin at the

    A.   front of the file and remove the cards one at a time, placing each one face up on top of the one removed before
    B.   front of the file and remove the cards one at a time, placing each one face down on top of the one removed before
    C.   back of the file and remove the cards in small groups, placing each group face down on top of the group removed before
    D.   back of the file and remove the cards one at a time, placing each one face up on top of the one removed before

11.____

12. A person would MOST likely make a *person-to-person* long distance telephone call when

    A.   he does not know whether the person to whom he wishes to speak is in
    B.   he wishes to speak to any person answering the telephone
    C.   he knows that the person to whom he wishes to speak will answer the telephone
    D.   the call is made before 7 P.M.

12. ____

13. In a certain file room, it is customary, when removing a record from the files, to insert an *out* card in its place. A clerk suggests keeping, in addition, a chronological list of all records removed and the names of the employees who have removed them.
This suggestion would be of GREATEST value

    A.   in avoiding duplication of work
    B.   in enabling an employee to refile records more easily
    C.   where records are frequently misfiled
    D.   where records are frequently kept out longer than necessary

13.____

14. You are given a large batch of correspondence and asked to obtain the folder on file for   14.____
each of the senders of these letters. The folders in your file room are kept in numerical
order and an alphabetic cross-index file is maintained.
Of the following, the BEST procedure would be for you to

  A. look up the numbers in the alphabetic file, then alphabetize the correspondence
  according to the senders' names and obtain the folders from the numerical file
  B. alphabetize the correspondence according to the senders' names, get the file numbers from the alphabetic file, and obtain the folders from the numerical file
  C. alphabetize the correspondence and then look through the numerical file for the
  proper folders in the order in which your correspondence is arranged
  D. look through the numerical file, pulling out the folders as you come across them

15. Designing forms of the proper size is of the utmost importance. Certain sizes are best   15.____
because they can be cut without waste from standard sheets of paper on which forms
are printed and because they fit standard files and binders.
The one of the following which is the MOST valid implication of the above passage is
that

  A. the size of a form should be decided upon before the information is printed on it
  B. the size of a form should be such that it can be printed on paper without cutting
  C. the person designing a form should be acquainted with standard sizes in file cabi-
  nets and paper
  D. the purpose of a form is an important factor in the determination of its size

16. When an employee is encouraged by his supervisor to think of new ideas in connection   16.____
with his work, the habit of improving work methods is fostered.
The one of the following which is the MOST valid implication of the above statement is
that

  A. the improvement of work methods should be the concern not only of the supervisor
  but of the employee as well
  B. an employee without initiative cannot perform his job well
  C. an employee may waste too much time in experimenting with new work methods
  D. an improved method for performing a task should not be used without the approval
  of the supervisor

17. The report on the work of the three employees furnishes definite proof that Jones is more   17.____
efficient than Smith, and that Brown is less efficient than Jones.
On the basis of the above information, the MOST accurate of the following statements
is that

  A. Brown is more efficient than Smith
  B. Smith is more efficient than Brown
  C. Smith is not necessarily less efficient than Jones
  D. Brown is not necessarily more efficient than Smith

18. Almost all students with a high school average of 80% or over were admitted to the col-   18.____
lege.
On the basis of this statement, it would be MOST accurate to assume that

A. a high school average of 80% or over was required for admittance to the college
B. some students with a high school average of less than 80% were admitted to the college
C. a high school average of at least 80% was desirable but not necessary for admission to the college
D. some students with a high school average of at least 80% were not admitted to the college

Questions 19-21.

DIRECTIONS: Questions 19 to 21 are to be answered SOLELY on the basis of the information contained in the following passage.

It is common knowledge that ability to do a particular job and performance on the job do not always go hand-in-hand. Persons with great potential abilities sometimes fall down on the job because of laziness or lack of interest in the job, while persons with mediocre talents have often achieved excellent results through their industry and their loyalty to the interests of their employers. It is clear, therefore, that in a balanced personnel program, measures of employee ability need to be supplemented by measures of employee performance, for the final test of any employee is his performance on the job.

19. The MOST accurate of the following statements, on the basis of the above paragraph, is that   19.____

    A. employees who lack ability are usually not industrious
    B. an employee's attitudes are more important than his abilities
    C. mediocre employees who are interested in their work are preferable to employees who possess great ability
    D. superior capacity for performance should be supplemented with proper attitudes

20. On the basis of the above paragraph, the employee of most value to his employer is NOT necessarily the one who   20.____

    A. best understands the significance of his duties
    B. achieves excellent results
    C. possesses the greatest talents
    D. produces the greatest amount of work

21. According to the above paragraph, an employee's efficiency is BEST determined by an   21.____

    A. appraisal of his interest in his work
    B. evaluation of the work performed by him
    C. appraisal of his loyalty to his employer
    D. evaluation of his potential ability to perform his work

22. Assume that you know the capacity of a filing cabinet, the extent of which it is filled, and the daily rate at which material is being added to the file.
In order to estimate how many more days it will take for the cabinet to be filled to capacity, you should   22.____

    A. divide the extent to which the cabinet is filled by the daily rate
    B. take the difference between the capacity of the cabinet and the material in it, and multiply the result by the daily rate of adding material

C. divide the daily rate of adding material by the difference between the capacity of the cabinet and the material in it

D. take the difference between the capacity of the cabinet and the material in it, and divide the result by the daily rate of adding material

23. Suppose you have been asked to compute the average salary earned in your depart-ment during the past year. For each of the divisions of the department, you are given the number of employees and the average salary.
In order to find the requested overall average salary for the department, you should

    23.___

    A. add the average salaries of the various divisions and divide the total by the number of divisions

    B. multiply the number of employees in each division by the corresponding average salary, add the results and divide the total by the number of employees in the department

    C. add the average salaries of the various divisions and divide the total by the total number of employees in the department

    D. multiply the sum of the average salaries of the various divisions by the total number of divisions and divide the resulting product by the total number of employees in the department

24. Three divisions within a department are working to complete a major six-month project with varying levels of responsibility. A manager asks you to prepare a chart or graph that indicates each division's share (by percentage) of the project's total expenses to date for review by a department supervisor. The most effective type of chart or graph to use in this case would be a

    24.___

    A. pie chart   B. line graph
    C. bar graph   D. Venn diagram

25. A study of the grades of students in a certain college revealed that in 2005, 15% fewer students received a passing grade in mathematics than in 2004, whereas in 2006, the number of students passing mathematics increased 15% over 2005.
On the basis of this study, it would be MOST accurate to conclude that

    25.___

    A. the same percentage of students passed mathematics in 2004 as in 2006

    B. of the three years studied, the greatest percentage of students passed mathemat-ics in 2006

    C. the percentage of students who passed mathematics in 2006 was less than the percentage passing this subject in 2004

    D. the percentage of students passing mathematics in 2004 was 15% greater than the percentage of students passing this subject in 2006

26. Some authority must determine finally whether constitutional guarantees mean literally and absolutely what they say, or something less or perchance more.
In the American system of government, that authority rests with the

    26.___

    A. elected representatives in Congress
    B. executive branch of the federal government
    C. courts
    D. state legislatures

27. Almost all city departments obtain their supplies and equipment through the Department of Purchase.
Of the following, the CHIEF justification for this procedure is to effect savings by means of

    A. large-scale consumption of standard office supplies
    B. competitive bidding
    C. centralized buying
    D. non-profit purchasing

27.____

28. The one of the following federal agencies which is MOST concerned with the conservation of natural resources in this country is the

    A. Department of Interior   B. Federal Trade Commission
    C. Department of Commerce   D. Department of State

28.____

29. A city employee who is familiar with economic affairs should know that a period of inflation can BEST be characterized as a period when

    A. there is universal prosperity
    B. savings can buy fewer things than anticipated
    C. the cost of necessities is high and the cost of luxuries is low
    D. the value of money is increased

29.____

30. A clerk interested in world affairs should know that UNESCO is concerned MAINLY with international cooperation

    A. in the control of atomic power
    B. in the relocation of refugees
    C. to raise health standards throughout the world
    D. through the free exchange of information on education, art, and science

30.__ __

31. Suppose that your supervisor gives you a folder of approximately 200 letters, arranged chronologically, and a list of the names of the writers of these letters, arranged alphabetically. He asks you to verify, without disarranging the order of the letters, that there is a letter in the folder for each name on the list. Of the following, the BEST procedure for you to follow is to

    A. glance at each of the letters in the folder in turn and place a light pencil check on the alphabetical list next to the name of the person writing that letter
    B. glance at each of the letters in the folder in turn and place a light pencil check on each letter if there is a corresponding name on the alphabetical list
    C. rearrange the letters in alphabetical order and verify that there is a one-to-one relationship between letters and names
    D. rewrite the names on the list in chronological order and verify that there is a one-to-one relationship between letters and names

31.____

32. Suppose that you will not be able to complete today an important job that you have been assigned and that you expect to be out of the office the next few days.
In general, the BEST action for you to take before leaving the office at the end of the day is to

    A. apportion the remainder of your work equally among the other clerks in your office
    B. arrange your work neatly on top of your desk

32.____

C. tell your supervisor exactly how much of the work you have been able to do
D. lock your work in your desk so that your work cannot be disturbed in your absence

33. Suppose that your supervisor has asked you to make a copy of a statistical table. 33._____
In general, the BEST method for checking the copy you prepare in order to make certain that the copy is absolutely accurate is for you to

   A. make a second copy of the table and compare the two copies
   B. have another clerk read the original table aloud to you while you read the copy
   C. compare all totals in the two tables, for if the totals check, the copy is probably accurate
   D. check the one or two points in the table at which an error is most likely to be made

34. Suppose that, in the course of your work, you frequently come into contact with the public. 34._____
The one of the following which is the BEST reason for courtesy in all your contacts with the public is that

   A. most individuals are fully aware of the methods and procedures of city departments
   B. some individuals who come to city agencies for information or assistance are so domineering in their attitude that it is difficult to be polite
   C. no employee of a private business organization would dare to be discourteous to a customer
   D. a favorable attitude on the part of the public toward civil service employees is necessary for maintenance of the merit system

35. *It is good office practice, when answering the telephone, to give immediately the name of* 35._____
the office in which you work.
Of the following, the BEST reason for following this practice is that it

   A. identifies immediately the particular person answering the telephone
   B. avoids loss of time due to mistaken or uncertain identity
   C. stimulates employees to answer the telephone quickly
   D. indicates directly that your supervisor is not in the office

Questions 36-44.

DIRECTIONS: Questions 36 to 44 consist of 9 groups of names. Consider each group of names as a unit. Determine in what position the name printed in ITALICS would be if the names in the group were CORRECTLY arranged in alphabetical order. If the name in italics should be first, print the letter A; if second, print the letter B; if third, print the letter C; if fourth, print the letter D; and if fifth, print the letter E. Indicate the answer in the space at the right. Below are some rules for alphabetizing which you are to use as a guide in answering these items:

   1. Arrange alphabetically, first, according to surnames; when surnames are the same, then according to given names or initials; when given names or initials are also the same, then according to middle names or initials.
   2. An initial precedes a name beginning with the same letter. For example: J. Martin precedes James Martin.

3. A name without a middle name or initial precedes the same name having a middle name or initial.
   For example: James Martin precedes James E. Martin.
4. Treat all abbreviations as if spelled out in full when the names for which they stand are commonly understood.
5. Arrange names beginning with "Mc" or "Mac" in their exact alphabetic order as spelled.
6. Treat names containing numerals as if numerals were spelled out.
7. The names of business organizations which do not include the name of a person are alphabetized as written, subject to the provisions of Rule 8.
8. Disregard the following in alphabetizing: the, and, titles and designations as Dr., Mr., Mrs., Jr., and Sr.

SAMPLE ITEM:

J.W. Martin	(2)
James E. Martin	(4)
J. Martin	(1)
George Martins	(5)
James Martin	(3)

The correct alphabetic order is indicated alongside the names in the sample item, and the correct answer should be D.

36. Albert Brown
    James Borenstein
    Frieda Albrecht
    Samuel Brown
    George Appelman

    36._____

37. James Ryn
    Francis Ryan
    Wm. Roanan
    Frances S. Ryan
    Francis P. Ryan

    37._____

38. Norman Fitzgibbons
    Charles F. Franklin
    Jas. Fitzgerald
    Andrew Fitzsimmons
    James P. Fitzgerald

    38._____

39. Hugh F. Martenson
    A.S. Martinson
    Albert Martinsen
    Albert S. Martinson
    M. Martanson

    39._____

40. Aaron M. Michelson
    Samuel Michels
    Arthur L. Michaelson, Sr.
    John Michell
    Daniel Michelsohn

    40._____

41. *Chas. R. Connolly*
    Frank Conlon
    Charles S. Connolly
    Abraham Cohen
    Chas. Conolly

41.____

42. James McCormack
    Ruth MacNamara
    Kathryn McGillicuddy
    Frances Mason
    Arthur MacAdams

42.____

43. Dr. Francis Karell
    John Joseph Karelsen, jr.
    John J. Karelsen, Sr.
    Mrs. Jeanette Kelly
    Estelle Karel

43.____

44. *The 5th Ave. Bus Co.*
    The Baltimore and Ohio Railroad
    3rd Ave. Elevated Co.
    The 4th Ave. Trolley Line

44.____

Questions 45-53.

DIRECTIONS: The following table contains certain information about employees in a city bureau. Questions 45 to 53 are to be answered on the basis of the facts given in this table.

RECORD OF EMPLOYEES IN A CITY BUREAU

NAME	TITLE	AGE	ANNUAL SALARY	YEARS OF SERVICE	EXAMINATION RATING
Jones	Clerk	34	$20,400	10	82
Smith	Stenographer	25	19,200	2	72
Black	Typist	19	14,400	1	71
Brown	Stenographer	36	25,200	12	88
Thomas	Accountant	49	41,200	21	91
Gordon	Clerk	31	30,000	8	81
Johnson	Stenographer	26	26,400	5	75
White	Accountant	53	36,000	30	90
Spencer	Clerk	42	27,600	19	85
Taylor	Typist	24	21,600	5	74
Simpson	Accountant	37	50,000	11	87
Reid	Typist	20	12,000	2	72
Fulton	Accountant	55	55,000	31	100
Chambers	Clerk	22	15,600	4	75
Calhoun	Stenographer	48	28,800	16	80

45. The name of the employee whose salary would be the middle one if all the salaries were ranked in order of magnitude is   45.____

    A. White   B. Johnson   C. Brown   D. Spencer

46. The combined monthly salary of all the stenographers exceeds the combined monthly salary of all the clerks by   46.____

    A. $6,000   B. $500   C. $22,800   D. $600

47. The age of the employee who received the HIGHEST rating in the examination among those who have less than 10 years of service is _____ years.   47.____

    A. 22   B. 31   C. 55   D. 34

48. The average examination rating of those employees who had 15 years of service or more as compared with the average examination rating of those employees who had 5 years of service or less is MOST NEARLY   48.____

    A. 16 points greater   B. 7 points greater
    C. 10 points less   D. 25 points greater

49. The name of the youngest employee whose monthly salary is more than $1,000 per month and who has more than one year of service is   49.____

    A. Reid   B. Black   C. Chambers   D. Taylor

50. The name of the employee who received an examination rating of over 85%, who has more than 15 years of service, and who earns a yearly salary of more than $25,000 but less than $40,000 is   50.____

    A. Thomas   B. Spencer   C. Calhoun   D. White

KEY (CORRECT ANSWERS)

1. D	11. A	21. B	31. A	41. C
2. C	12. A	22. D	32. C	42. C
3. C	13. D	23. B	33. B	43. D
4. D	14. B	24. A	34. D	44. B
5. A	15. C	25. A	35. B	45. B
6. B	16. A	26. C	36. E	46. B
7. C	17. D	27. C	37. D	47. B
8. B	18. D	28. A	38. A	48. A
9. A	19. D	29. B	39. E	49. C
10. B	20. C	30. D	40. D	50. D

TEST 2

DIRECTIONS: Each question or incomplete statement is followed by several suggested answers or completions. Select the one that BEST answers the question or completes the statement. *PRINT THE LETTER OF THE CORRECT ANSWER IN THE SPACE AT THE RIGHT.*

1. The annual salary of the HIGHEST paid stenographer is   1.____

   A. more than twice as great as the salary of the youngest employee
   B. greater than the salary of the oldest typist but not as great as the salary of the oldest clerk
   C. greater than the salary of the highest paid typist but not as great as the salary of the lowest paid accountant
   D. less than the combined salaries of the two youngest typists

2. The number of employees whose annual salary is more than $15,600 but less than $28,800 and who have at least 5 years of service is   2.____

   A. 11   B. 8   C. 6   D. 5

3. Of the following, it would be MOST accurate to state that the   3.____

   A. youngest employee is lowest with respect to number of years of service, examination rating, and salary
   B. oldest employee is highest with respect to number of years of service, examination rating, but not with respect to salary
   C. annual salary of the youngest clerk is $1,200 more than the annual salary of the youngest typist and $2,400 less than the annual salary of the youngest stenographer
   D. difference in age between the youngest and oldest typist is less than one-fourth the difference in age between the youngest and oldest stenographer

4. *He advocated a new course of action.* The word *advocated* means MOST NEARLY   4.____

   A. described   B. refused to discuss
   C. argued against   D. supported

5. A clerk who is assigned to make a *facsimile* of a report should make a copy which is   5.____

   A. exact   B. larger   C. smaller   D. edited

6. *A city employee must be a person of integrity.* The word *integrity* means MOST NEARLY   6.____

   A. intelligence   B. competence
   C. honesty   D. keenness

7. A person who displays *apathy* is   7.____

   A. irritated   B. confused
   C. indifferent   D. insubordinate

8. *The supervisor admonished the clerk for his tardiness.* The word *admonished* means MOST NEARLY   8.____

   A. reproved   B. excused   C. transferred   D. punished

9. A *lucrative* business is one which is   9._____

    A. unprofitable   B. gainful   C. unlawful   D. speculative

10. To say that the work is *tedious* means MOST NEARLY that it is   10._____

    A. technical   B. interesting
    C. tiresome   D. confidential

11. A *vivacious* person is one who is   11._____

    A. kind   B. talkative   C. lively   D. well-dressed

12. An *innocuous* statement is one which is   12._____

    A. forceful   B. harmless   C. offensive   D. brief

13. To say that the order was *rescinded* means MOST NEARLY that it was   13._____

    A. revised   B. canceled
    C. misinterpreted   D. confirmed

14. To say that the administrator *amplified* his remarks means MOST NEARLY that the remarks were   14._____

    A. shouted   B. expanded
    C. carefully analyzed   D. summarized briefly

15. *Peremptory commands will be resented in any office.* The word *peremptory* means MOST NEARLY   15._____

    A. unexpected   B. unreasonable
    C. military   D. dictatorial

16. A clerk should know that the word *sporadic* means MOST NEARLY   16._____

    A. occurring regularly   B. sudden
    C. scattered   D. disturbing

17. To *vacillate* means MOST NEARLY to   17._____

    A. lubricate   B. waver   C. decide   D. investigate

18. A *homogeneous* group of persons is characterized by its   18._____

    A. similarity   B. teamwork
    C. discontent   D. differences

19. A *vindictive* person is one who is   19._____

    A. prejudiced   B. unpopular   C. petty   D. revengeful

20. The abbreviation *e.g.* occurs frequently in written matter and is commonly taken to mean   20._____

    A. note carefully   B. for example
    C. entire group   D. and others

21. The abbreviation *i.e.* also occurs frequently in written matter and is commonly taken to mean   21._____

    A. that is   B. the same
    C. in the same place   D. and others

Questions 22-37.

DIRECTIONS: Each of the sentences numbered 22 to 37 may be classified MOST appropriately under one of the following four categories:
- A. faulty because of incorrect grammar
- B. faulty because of incorrect punctuation
- C. faulty because of incorrect capitalization
- D. correct

Examine each sentence carefully. Then, in the correspondingly numbered space at the right, print the letter preceding the option which is the BEST of the four suggested above. All incorrect sentences contain but one type of error. Consider a sentence correct if it contains none of the types of errors mentioned, even though there may be other correct ways of expressing the same thought.

22.   The desk, as well as the chairs, were moved out of the office.   22._____

23.   The clerk whose production was greatest for the month won a day's vacation as first prize.   23._____

24.   Upon entering the room, the employees were found hard at work at their desks.   24._____

25.   John Smith our new employee always arrives at work on time.   25._____

26.   Punish whoever is guilty of stealing the money.   26._____

27.   Intelligent and persistent effort lead to success no matter what the job may be.   27._____

28.   The secretary asked, "can you call again at three o'clock?"   28._____

29.   He told us, that if the report was not accepted at the next meeting, it would have to be rewritten.   29._____

30.   He would not have sent the letter if he had known that it would cause so much excitement.   30._____

31.   We all looked forward to him coming to visit us.   31._____

32.   If you find that you are unable to complete the assignment please notify me as soon as possible.   32._____

33.   Every girl in the office went home on time but me; there was still some work for me to finish.   33._____

34.   He wanted to know who the letter was addressed to, Mr. Brown or Mr. Smith.   34._____

35.   "Mr. Jones, he said, please answer this letter as soon as possible."   35._____

36.   The new clerk had an unusual accent inasmuch as he was born and educated in the south.   36._____

37.   Although he is younger than her, he earns a higher salary.   37._____

Questions 38-45.

DIRECTIONS: Questions 38 to 45 consist of four words each. In each item, one of the words may be spelled incorrectly or all the words may be spelled correctly. If one of the words in an item is spelled incorrectly, print in the correspondingly numbered space at the right the letter preceding the word which is spelled incorrectly. If all four words are spelled correctly, print the letter E.

38.	A. temporary	B. existance	C. complimentary	D. altogether	38. _B_
39.	A. privilege	B. changeable	C. jeopardize	D. commitment	39. _E_
40.	A. grievous	B. alloted	C. outrageous	D. mortgage	40. _B_
41.	A. tempermental B. accommodating		B. bookkeeping D. panicky		41. _E_
42.	A. auxiliary	B. indispensable	C. ecstasy	D. fiery	42. _A_
43.	A. dissapear	B. buoyant	C. imminent	D. parallel	43. _A_
44.	A. loosly	B. medicine	C. schedule	D. defendant	44. _A_
45.	A. endeavor	B. persuade	C. retroactive	D. desparate	45. _D_

Questions 46-50

DIRECTIONS: Each of Questions 46 to 50 contains five words in italics, one of which is not in keeping with the meaning which the question is evidently intended to carry. The five words in italics in each item are reprinted after the question. On the correspondingly numbered space at the right, print the letter preceding the one of the five words which does MOST to spoil the true meaning of the question.

46. City departments having direct *contact* with the *public* should be located *if* they are readily *accessible* to those *coming* to the office on business.

    A. contact   B. public   C. if
    D. accessible   E. coming

46. _____

47. Many communications covering a *specific* subject can be form letters, but going to *extremes* in this matter should be guarded against; to send a form letter when a specially *composed* letter should be used is *often* the most mistaken *extravagance.*

    A. specific   B. extremes   C. composed
    D. often   E. extravagance

47. _____

48. In order to prevent *unavoidable* accidents, a *safety* engineer designs and superintends the *installation* of safety devices. If employees always used the safety devices *provided,* there would be *few* accidents.

    A. unavoidable   B. safety   C. installation
    D. provided   E. few

48. _____

49. Most business records have an intangible *value* to the business which *can* be measured 49.____
in dollars and cents. They are the *result* of figures and facts obtained from many sources
and are often *impossible* to replace at *any* cost of time or money.

   A. value   B. can   C. result   D. impossible E. any

50. A major advantage gained by a company that uses only one *particular* type of a machine 50.____
is greater *efficiency* of operation. If, for example, all the calculating machines in an office
are identical, it is *trifling* that time is *saved* by employees in *learning* how to operate these
machines.

   A. particular   B. efficiency   C. trifling
   D. saved   E. learning

KEY (CORRECT ANSWERS)

1. C	11. C	21. A	31. A	41. A
2. D	12. B	22. A	32. B	42. E
3. D	13. B	23. D	33. D	43. A
4. D	14. B	24. A	34. A	44. A
5. A	15. D	25. B	35. B	45. D
6. C	16. C	26. D	36. C	46. C
7. C	17. B	27. A	37. A	47. E
8. A	18. A	28. C	38. B	48. A
9. B	19. D	29. A	39. E	49. B
10. C	20. B	30. D	40. B	50. C

CLERICAL ABILITIES TEST

EXAMINATION SECTION
TEST 1

DIRECTIONS: Each question or incomplete statement is followed by several suggested answers or completions. Select the one that *BEST* answers the question or completes the statement. *PRINT THE LETTER OF THE CORRECT ANSWER IN THE SPACE AT THE RIGHT.*

Questions 1-10.

DIRECTIONS: Questions 1 through 10 consist of lines of names, dates and numbers. For each question, you are to choose the option (A, B, C, or D) in Column II which *EXACTLY* matches the information in Column I. *PRINT THE LETTER OF THE CORRECT ANSWER IN THE SPACE AT THE RIGHT.*

SAMPLE QUESTION

Column I		Column II		
Schneider 11/16/75 581932	A.	Schneider	11/16/75	518932
	B.	Schneider	11/16/75	581932
	C.	Schnieder	11/16/75	581932
	D.	Shnieder	11/16/75	518932

The correct answer is B. Only option B shows the name, date and number exactly as they are in Column I. Option A has a mistake in the number. Option C has a mistake in the name. Option D has a mistake in the name and in the number. Now answer Questions 1 through 10 in the same manner.

	Column I		Column II	
1.	Johnston 12/26/74 659251	A.	Johnson 12/23/74 659251	1._____
		B.	Johston 12/26/74 659251	
		C.	Johnston 12/26/74 695251	
		D.	Johnston 12/26/74 659251	
2.	Allison 1/26/75 9939256	A.	Allison 1/26/75 9939256	2._____
		B.	Alisson 1/26/75 9939256	
		C.	Allison 1/26/76 9399256	
		D.	Allison 1/26/75 9993256	
3.	Farrell 2/12/75 361251	A.	Farell 2/21/75 361251	3._____
		B.	Farrell 2/12/75 361251	
		C.	Farrell 2/21/75 361251	
		D.	Farrell 2/12/75 361151	
4.	Guerrero 4/28/72 105689	A.	Guererro 4/28/72 105689	4._____
		B.	Guererro 4/28/72 105986	
		C.	Guerrero 4/28/72 105869	
		D.	Guerrero 4/28/72 105689	

5. McDonnell 6/05/73 478215

    A. McDonnell 6/15/73 478215
    B. McDonnell 6/05/73 478215
    C. McDonnell 6/05/73 472815
    D. MacDonell 6/05/73 478215

    5.____

6. Shepard 3/31/71 075421

    A. Sheperd 3/31/71 075421
    B. Shepard 3/13/71 075421
    C. Shepard 3/31/71 075421
    D. Shepard 3/13/71 075241

    6.____

7. Russell 4/01/69 031429

    A. Russell 4/01/69 031429
    B. Russell 4/10/69 034129
    C. Russell 4/10/69 031429
    D. Russell 4/01/69 034129

    7.____

8. Phillips 10/16/68 961042

    A. Philipps 10/16/68 961042
    B. Phillips 10/16/68 960142
    C. Phillips 10/16/68 961042
    D. Philipps 10/16/68 916042

    8.____

9. Campbell 11/21/72 624856

    A. Campbell 11/21/72 624856
    B. Campbell 11/21/72 624586
    C. Campbell 11/21/72 624686
    D. Campbel 11/21/72 624856

    9.____

10. Patterson 9/18/71 76199176

    A. Patterson 9/18/72 76191976
    B. Patterson 9/18/71 76199176
    C. Patterson 9/18/72 76199176
    D. Patterson 9/18/71 76919176

    10.____

Questions 11-15.

DIRECTIONS: Questions 11 through 15 consist of groups of numbers and letters which you are to compare. For each question, you are to choose the option (A, B, C, or D) in Column II which *EXACTLY* matches the group of numbers and letters given in Column I.

SAMPLE QUESTION

Column I
B92466

Column II
A. B92644
B. B94266
C. A92466
D. B92466

The correct answer is D. Only option D in Column II shows the group of numbers and letters *EXACTLY* as it appears in Column I. Now answer Questions 11 through 15 in the same manner.

Column I

11.   925AC5

Column II
A. 952CA5
B. 925AC5
C. 952AC5
D. 925CA6

12.   Y006925

    A. Y060925
    B. Y006295
    C. Y006529
    D. Y006925

13.   J236956

    A. J236956
    B. J326965
    C. J239656
    D. J932656

14.   AB6952

    A. AB6952
    B. AB9625
    C. AB9652
    D. AB6925

15.   X259361

    A. X529361
    B. X259631
    C. X523961
    D. X259361

Questions 16-25.

DIRECTIONS: Each of Questions 16 through 25 consists of three lines of code letters and three lines of numbers. The numbers on each line should correspond with the code letters on the same line in accordance with the table below.

Code Letter	S	V	W	A	Q	M	X	E	G	K
Corresponding Number	0	1	2	3	4	5	6	7	8	9

On some of the lines, an error exists in the coding. Compare the letters and numbers in each question carefully. If you find an error or errors on:

    only *one* of the lines in the question, mark your answer A;
    any *two* lines in the question, mark your answer B;
    all *three* lines in the question, mark your answer C;
    none of the lines in the question, mark your answer D.

SAMPLE QUESTION

WQGKSXG   2489068
XEKVQMA   6591453
KMAESXV   9527061

In the above example, the first line is correct since each code letter listed has the correct corresponding number. On the second line, an error exists because code letter E should have the number 7 instead of the number 5. On the third line an error exists because the code letter A should have the number 3 instead of the number 2. Since there are errors in two of the three lines, the correct answer is B. Now answer Questions 16 through 25 in the same manner.

16.   SWQEKGA   0247983   16._____
      KEAVSXM   9731065
      SSAXGKQ   0036894

17.   QAMKMVS   4259510   17._____
      MGGEASX   5897306
      KSWMKWS   9125920

18. WKXQWVE   2964217   18.____
      QKXXQVA   4966413
      AWMXGVS   3253810

19. GMMKASE   8559307   19.____
      AWVSKSW   3210902
      QAVSVGK   4310189

20. XGKQSMK   6894049   20.____
      QSVKEAS   4019730
      GSMXKMV   8057951

21. AEKMWSG   3195208   21.____
      MKQSVQK   5940149
      XGQAEVW   6843712

22. XGMKAVS   6858310   22.____
      SKMAWEQ   0953174
      GVMEQSA   8167403

23. VQSKAVE   1489317   23.____
      WQGKAEM   2489375
      MEGKAWQ   5689324

24. XMQVSKG   6541098   24.____
      QMEKEWS   4579720
      KMEVKGA   9571983

25. GKVAMEW   8912572   25.____
      AXMVKAE   3651937
      KWAGMAV   9238531

Questions 26-35.

DIRECTIONS: Each of Questions 26 through 35 consists of a column of figures. For each question, add the column of figures and choose the correct answer from the four choices given.

26.   5,665.43   26.____
      2,356.69
      6,447.24
      <u>7,239.65</u>

      A.   20,698.01   B.   21,709.01
      C.   21,718.01   D.   22,609.01

27.   817,209.55   27.____
      264,354.29
       82,368.76
      <u>849,964.89</u>

      A.   1,893,997.49   B.   1,989,988.39
      C.   2,009,077.39   D.   2,013,897,49

28. 156,366.89
    249,973.23
    823,229.49
    56,869.45

    A. 1,286,439.06   B. 1,287,521.06
    C. 1,297,539.06   D. 1,296,421.06

28.____

29. 23,422.15
    149,696.24
    238,377.53
    86,289.79
    505,544.63

    A. 989,229.34   B. 999,879.34
    C. 1,003,330.34   D. 1,023,329.34

29.____

30. 2,468,926.70
    656,842.28
    49,723.15
    832,369.59

    A. 3,218,061.72   B. 3,808,092.72
    C. 4,007,861.72   D. 4,818,192.72

30.____

31. 524,201.52
    7,775,678.51
    8,345,299.63
    40,628,898.08
    31,374,670.07

    A. 88,646,647.81   B. 88,646,747.91
    C. 88,648,647.91   D. 88,648,747.81

31.____

32. 6,824,829.40
    682,482.94
    5,542,015.27
    775,678.51
    7,732,507.25

    A. 21,557,513.37   B. 21,567,513.37
    C. 22,567,503.37   D. 22,567,513.37

32.____

33. 22,109,405.58
    6,097,093.43
    5,050,073.99
    8,118,050.05
    4,313,980.82

    A. 45,688,593.87   B. 45,688,603.87
    C. 45,689,593.87   D. 45,689,603.87

33.____

34. 79,324,114.19
    99,848,129.74
    43,331,653.31
    41,610,207.14

34.____

A. 264,114,104.38   B. 264,114,114.38
C. 265,114,114.38   D. 265,214,104.38

35.   33,729,653.94   35.___
         5,959,342.58
        26,052,715.47
         4,452,669.52
         7,079,953.59

A. 76,374,334.10   B. 76,375,334.10
C. 77,274,335.10   D. 77,275,335.10

Questions 36-40.

DIRECTIONS: Each of Questions 36 through 40 consists of a single number in Column I and
              four options in Column II. For each question, you are to choose the option (A,
              B, C, or D) in Column II which *EXACTLY* matches the number in Column I.
                              SAMPLE QUESTION

Column I   Column II
5965121   A.   5956121
                          B.   5965121
                          C.   5966121
                          D.   5965211

The correct answer is B. Only option B shows the number *EXACTLY* as it appears in Column I.
Now answer Questions 36 through 40 in the same manner.

Column I   Column II
36. 9643242   A.   9643242
                          B.   9462342
                          C.   9642442
                          D.   9463242

37. 3572477   A.   3752477
                          B.   3725477
                          C.   3572477
                          D.   3574277

38. 5276101   A.   5267101
                          B.   5726011
                          C.   5271601
                          D.   5276101

39. 4469329   A.   4496329
                          B.   4469329
                          C.   4496239
                          D.   4469239

40. 2326308   A.   2236308
                          B.   2233608
                          C.   2326308
                          D.   2323608

KEY (CORRECT ANSWERS)

1.	D	11.	B	21.	A	31.	D
2.	A	12.	D	22.	C	32.	A
3.	B	13.	A	23.	B	33.	B
4.	D	14.	A	24.	D	34.	A
5.	B	15.	D	25.	A	35.	C
6.	C	16.	D	26.	B	36.	A
7.	A	17.	C	27.	D	37.	C
8.	C	18.	A	28.	A	38.	D
9.	A	19.	D	29.	C	39.	B
10.	B	20.	B	30.	C	40.	C

TEST 2

Questions 1-5.

DIRECTIONS: Each of Questions 1 through 5 consists of a name and a dollar amount. In each question, the name and dollar amount in Column II should be an exact copy of the name and dollar amount in Column I. If there is:

a mistake only in the name, mark your answer A;
a mistake only in the dollar amount, mark your answer B;
a mistake in both the name and the dollar amount, mark your answer C;
no mistake in either the name or the dollar amount, mark your answer D.

SAMPLE QUESTION

Column I	Column II
George Peterson	George Petersson
$125.50	$125.50

Compare the name and dollar amount in Column II with the name and dollar amount in Column I. The name *Petersson* in Column II is spelled *Peterson* in Column I. The amount is the same in both columns. Since there is a mistake only in the name, the answer to the sample question is A.

Now answer Questions 1 through 5 in the same manner.

	Column I	Column II	
1.	Susanne Shultz $3440	Susanne Schultz $3440	1._____
2.	Anibal P. Contrucci $2121.61	Anibel P. Contrucci $2112.61	2._____
3.	Eugenio Mendoza $12.45	Eugenio Mendozza $12.45	3._____
4.	Maurice Gluckstadt $4297	Maurice Gluckstadt $4297	4._____
5.	John Pampellonne $4656.94	John Pammpellonne $4566.94	5._____

Questions 6-11.

DIRECTIONS: Each of Questions 6 through 11 consists of a set of names and addresses which you are to compare. In each question, the name and addresses in Column II should be an *EXACT* copy of the name and address in Column I. If there is:

a mistake only in the name, mark your answer A;
a mistake only in the address, mark your answer B;
a mistake in both the name and address, mark your answer C;
no mistake in either the name or address, mark your answer D.

SAMPLE QUESTION

Column I	Column II
Michael Filbert	Michael Filbert
456 Reade Street	645 Reade Street
New York, N.	New York, N . Y. 10013

Since there is a mistake only in the address (the street number should be 456 instead of 645), the answer to the sample question is B.

Now answer Questions 6 through 11 in the same manner.

	Column I	Column II	

6. Hilda Goettelmann   Hilda Goettelman   6.____
   55 Lenox Rd.   55 Lenox Ave.
   Brooklyn, N. Y. 11226   Brooklyn, N. Y. 11226

7. Arthur Sherman   Arthur Sharman   7.____
   2522 Batchelder St.   2522 Batcheder St.
   Brooklyn, N. Y. 11235   Brooklyn, N. Y. 11253

8. Ralph Barnett   Ralph Barnett   8.____
   300 West 28 Street   300 West 28 Street
   New York, New York 10001   New York, New York 10001

9. George Goodwin   George Godwin   9.____
   135 Palmer Avenue   135 Palmer Avenue
   Staten Island, New York 10302   Staten Island, New York 10302

10. Alonso Ramirez   Alonso Ramirez   10.____
    232 West 79 Street   223 West 79 Street
    New York, N. Y. 10024   New York, N. Y. 10024

11. Cynthia Graham   Cynthia Graham   11.____
    149-35 83 Street   149-35 83 Street
    Howard Beach, N. Y. 11414   Howard Beach, N. Y. 11414

Questions 12-20.

DIRECTIONS: Questions 12 through 20 are problems in subtraction. For each question do the subtraction and select your answer from the four choices given.

12.   232,921.85   12.____
    -179,587.68

    A. 52,433.17   B. 52,434.17
    C. 53,334.17   D. 53,343.17

13.   5,531,876.29   13.____
    -3,897,158.36

    A. 1,634,717.93   B. 1,644,718.93
    C. 1,734,717.93   D. 1,734,718.93

14. 1,482,658.22   14.____
    - 937,925.76

    A. 544,633.46   B. 544,732.46
    C. 545,632.46   D. 545,732.46

15.   937,828.17   15.____
    -259,673.88

    A. 678,154.29   B. 679,154.29
    C. 688,155.39   D. 699,155.39

16.   760,412.38
     -263,465.95

     A. 496,046.43   B. 496,946.43
     C. 496,956.43   D. 497,046.43

16.__

17.   3,203,902.26
     -2,933,087.96

     A. 260,814.30   B. 269,824.30
     C. 270,814.30   D. 270,824.30

17.__

18.   1,023,468.71
     - 934,678.88

     A. 88,780.83   B. 88,789.83
     C. 88,880.83   D. 88,889.83

18.__

19.   831,549.47
     -772,814.78

     A. 58,734.69   B. 58,834.69
     C. 59,735,69   D. 59,834.69

19.__

20.   6,306,281.74
     -3,617,376.75

     A. 2,687,904.99   B. 2,688,904.99
     C. 2,689,804.99   D. 2,799,905.99

20.__

Questions 21-30.

DIRECTIONS: Each of Questions 21 through 30 consists of three lines of code letters and three lines of numbers. The numbers on each line should correspond with the code letters on the same line in accordance with the table below.

Code Letter	J	U	B	T	Y	D	K	R	L	P
Corresponding Number	0	1	2	3	4	5	6	7	8	9

On some of the lines, an error exists in the coding. Compare the letters and numbers in each question carefully. If you find an error or errors on:

    only *one* of the lines in the question, mark your answer A;
    any *two* lines in the question, mark your answer B;
    all *three* lines in the question, mark your answer C;
    none of the lines in the question, mark your answer D.

SAMPLE QUESTION

BJRPYUR   2079417
DTBPYKJ   5328460
YKLDBLT   4685283

In the above sample the first line is correct since each code letter listed has the correct corresponding number. On the second line, an error exists because code letter P should have the number 9 instead of the number 8. The third line is correct since each code letter listed has the correct corresponding number. Since there is an error in *one* of the three lines, the correct answer is A.

Now answer Questions 21 through 30 in the same manner.

21.	BYPDTJL	2495308	21.____
	PLRDTJU	9815301	
	DTJRYLK	5207486	
22.	RPBYRJK	7934706	22.____
	PKTYLBU	9624821	
	KDLPJYR	6489047	
23.	TPYBUJR	3942107	23.____
	BYRKPTU	2476931	
	DUKPYDL	5169458	
24.	KBYDLPL	6345898	24.____
	BLRKBRU	2876261	
	JTULDYB	0318542	
25.	LDPYDKR	8594567	25.____
	BDKDRJL	2565708	
	BDRPLUJ	2679810	
26.	PLRLBPU	9858291	26.____
	LPYKRDJ	8936750	
	TDKPDTR	3569527	
27.	RKURPBY	7617924	27.____
	RYUKPTJ	7426930	
	RTKPTJD	7369305	
28.	DYKPBJT	5469203	28.____
	KLPJBTL	6890238	
	TKPLBJP	3698209	
29.	BTPRJYL	2397148	29.____
	LDKUTYR	8561347	
	YDBLRPJ	4528190	
30.	ULPBKYT	1892643	30.____
	KPDTRBJ	6953720	
	YLKJPTB	4860932	

KEY (CORRECT ANSWERS)

1.	A		16.	B
2.	C		17.	C
3.	A		18.	B
4.	D		19.	A
5.	C		20.	B
6.	C		21.	B
7.	C		22.	C
8.	D		23.	D
9.	A		24.	B
10.	B		25.	A
11.	D		26.	C
12.	C		27.	A
13.	A		28.	D
14.	B		29.	B
15.	A		30.	D

NAME and NUMBER COMPARISONS

COMMENTARY

This test seeks to measure your ability and disposition to do a job carefully and accurately, your attention to exactness and preciseness of detail, your alertness and versatility in discerning similarities and differences between things, and your power in systematically handling written language symbols.

It is actually a test of your ability to do academic and/or clerical work, using the basic elements of verbal (qualitative) and mathematical (quantitative) learning - words and numbers.

EXAMINATION SECTION
TEST 1

DIRECTIONS: In each line across the page there are three names or numbers that are much alike. Compare the three names or numbers and decide which ones are exactly alike. *PRINT IN THE SPACE AT THE RIGHT THE LETTER:*
A.   if all THREE names or numbers are exactly ALIKE
B.   if only the FIRST and SECOND names or numbers are ALIKE
C.   if only the FIRST and THIRD names or numbers are ALIKE
D.   if only the SECOND and THIRD names or numbers are ALIKE
E.   if ALL THREE names or numbers are DIFFERENT

1. Davis Hazen	David Hozen	David Hazen	1.____
2. Lois Appel	Lois Appel	Lois Apfel	2.____
3. June Allan	Jane Allan	Jane Allan	3.____
4. 10235	10235	10235	4.____
5. 32614	32164	32614	5.____

TEST 2

1. 2395890	2395890	2395890	1.____
2. 1926341	1926347	1926314	2.____
3. E. Owens McVey	E. Owen McVey	E. Owen McVay	3.____
4. Emily Neal Rouse	Emily Neal Rowse	Emily Neal Rowse	4.____
5. H. Merritt Audubon	H. Merriott Audubon	H. Merritt Audubon	5.____

TEST 3

1.	6219354	6219354	6219354	1.___
2.	2312793	2312793	2312793	2.___
3.	1065407	1065407	1065047	3.___
4.	Francis Ransdell	Frances Ramsdell	Francis Ramsdell	4.___
5.	Cornelius Detwiler	Cornelius Detwiler	Cornelius Detwiler	5.___

TEST 4

1.	6452054	6452654	6542054	1.___
2.	8501268	8501268	8501286	2.___
3.	Ella Burk Newham	Ella Burk Newnham	Elena Burk Newnham	3.___
4.	Jno. K. Ravencroft	Jno. H. Ravencroft	Jno. H. Ravencoft	4.___
5.	Martin Wills Pullen	Martin Wills Pulen	Martin Wills Pullen	5.___

TEST 5

1.	3457988	3457986	3457986	1.___
2.	4695682	4695862	4695682	2.___
3.	Stricklund Kaneydy	Sticklund Kanedy	Stricklund Kanedy	3.___
4.	Joy Harlor Witner	Joy Harloe Witner	Joy Harloe Witner	4.___
5.	R.M.O. Uberroth	R.M.O. Uberroth	R.N.O. Uberroth	5.___

2

TEST 6

1. 1592514	1592574	1592574	1._____
2. 2010202	2010202	2010220	2._____
3. 6177396	6177936	6177396	3._____
4. Drusilla S. Ridgeley	Drusilla S. Ridgeley	Drusilla S. Ridgeley	4._____
5. Andrei I. Toumantzev	Andrei I. Tourmantzev	Andrei I. Toumantzov	5._____

TEST 7

1. 5261383	5261383	5261338	1._____
2. 8125690	8126690	8125609	2._____
3. W.E. Johnston	W.E. Johnson	W.E. Johnson	3._____
4. Vergil L. Muller	Vergil L. Muller	Vergil L. Muller	4._____
5. Atherton R. Warde	Asheton R. Warde	Atherton P. Warde	5._____

TEST 8

1. 013469.5	023469.5	02346.95	1._____
2. 33376	333766	333766	2._____
3. Ling-Temco-Vought	Ling-Tenco-Vought	Ling-Temco Vought	3._____
4. Lorilard Corp.	Lorillard Corp.	Lorrilard Corp.	4._____
5. American Agronomics Corporation	American Agronomics Corporation	American Agronomic Corporation	5._____

TEST 9

1.	436592864	436592864	436592864	1.____
2.	197765123	197755123	197755123	2.____
3.	Dewaay, Cortvriendt International S.A.	Deway, Cortvriendt International S.A.	Deway, Corturiendt International S.A.	3.____
4.	Credit Lyonnais	Credit Lyonnais	Credit Lyonais	4.____
5.	Algemene Bank Nederland N.V.	Algamene Bank Nederland N.V.	Algemene Bank Naderland N.V.	5.____

TEST 10

1.	00032572	0.0032572	00032522	1.____
2.	399745	399745	398745	2.____
3.	Banca Privata Finanziaria S.p.A.	Banca Privata Finanzaria S.P.A.	Banca Privata Finanziaria S.P.A.	3.____
4.	Eastman Dillon, Union Securities & Co.	Eastman Dillon, Union Securities Co.	Eastman Dillon, Union Securities & Co.	4.____
5.	Arnhold and S. Bleichroeder, Inc.	Arnhold & S. Bleichroeder, Inc.	Arnold and S. Bleichroeder, Inc.	5.____

TEST 11

DIRECTIONS: Answer the questions below on the basis of the following instructions: For each such numbered set of names, addresses and numbers listed in Columns I and II, select your answer from the following options:

    A: The names in Columns I and II are different
    B: The addresses in Columns I and II are different
    C: The numbers in Columns I and II are different
    D: The names, addresses and numbers are identical

1.   Francis Jones   Francis Jones   1.____
         62 Stately Avenue   62 Stately Avenue
         96-12446   96-21446

2.   Julio Montez   Julio Montez   2.____
         19 Ponderosa Road   19 Ponderosa Road
         56-73161   56-71361

3.   Mary Mitchell   Mary Mitchell   3.____
         2314 Melbourne Drive   2314 Melbourne Drive
         68-92172   68-92172

4.   Harry Patterson   Harry Patterson   4.____
         25 Dunne Street   25 Dunne Street
         14-33430   14-34330

5.   Patrick Murphy   Patrick Murphy   5.____
         171 West Hosmer Street   171 West Hosmer Street
         93-81214   93-18214

TEST 12

1.   August Schultz   August Schultz   1.____
         816 St. Clair Avenue   816 St. Claire Avenue
         53-40149   53-40149

2.   George Taft   George Taft   2.____
         72 Runnymede Street   72 Runnymede Street
         47-04033   47-04023

3.   Angus Henderson   Angus Henderson   3.____
         1418 Madison Street   1418 Madison Street
         81-76375   81-76375

4.   Carolyn Mazur   Carolyn Mazur   4.____
         12 Riven/lew Road   12 Rivervane Road
         38-99615   38-99615

5.   Adele Russell   Adela Russell   5.____
         1725 Lansing Lane   1725 Lansing Lane
         72-91962   72-91962

TEST 13

DIRECTIONS: The following questions are based on the instructions given below. In each of the following questions, the 3-line name and address in Column I is the master-list entry, and the 3-line entry in Column II is the information to be checked against the master list.

    If there is one line that is *not* exactly alike, mark your answer A.
    If there are two lines *not* exactly alike, mark your answer B.
    If there are three lines *not* exactly alike, mark your answer C.
    If the lines *all are* exactly alike, mark your answer D.

1.   Jerome A. Jackson   Jerome A. Johnson   1.____
          1243 14th Avenue   1234 14th Avenue
          New York, N.Y. 10023   New York, N.Y. 10023

2.   Sophie Strachtheim   Sophie Strachtheim   2.____
          33-28 Connecticut Ave.   33-28 Connecticut Ave.
          Far Rockaway, N.Y. 11697 Far Rockaway, N.Y. 11697

3.   Elisabeth NT. Gorrell   Elizabeth NT. Gorrell   3.____
          256 Exchange St   256 Exchange St.
          New York, N.Y. 10013   New York, N.Y. 10013

4.   Maria J. Gonzalez   Maria J. Gonzalez   4.____
          7516 E. Sheepshead Rd.   7516 N. Shepshead Rd.
          Brooklyn, N.Y. 11240   Brooklyn, N.Y. 11240

5.   Leslie B. Brautenweiler   Leslie B. Brautenwieler   5.____
          21-57A Seller Terr.   21-75ASeilerTerr.
          Flushing, N.Y. 11367   Flushing, N.J. 11367

KEYS (CORRECT ANSWERS)

TEST 1		TEST 2		TEST 3		TEST 4		TEST 5		TEST 6		TEST 7	
1.	E	1.	A	1.	A	1.	E	1.	D	1.	D	1.	B
2.	B	2.	E	2.	A	2.	B	2.	C	2.	B	2.	E
3.	D	3.	E	3.	B	3.	E	3.	E	3.	C	3.	D
4.	A	4.	D	4.	E	4.	E	4.	D	4.	A	4.	A
5.	C	5.	C	5.	A	5.	C	5.	B	5.	E	5.	E

TEST 8		TEST 9		TEST 10		TEST 11		TEST 12		TEST 13	
1.	E	1.	A	1.	E	1.	C	1.	B	1.	B
2.	D	2.	D	2.	B	2.	C	2.	C	2.	D
3.	E	3.	E	3.	E	3.	D	3.	D	3.	A
4.	E	4.	E	4.	C	4.	C	4.	B	4.	A
5.	B	5.	E	5.	E	5.	C	5.	A	5.	C

FILING

EXAMINATION SECTION
TEST 1

DIRECTIONS: Questions 1 through 8 each show in Column I names written on four cards (lettered w, x, y, z) which have to be filed. You are to choose the option (lettered A, B, C, or D) in Column II which *BEST* represents the proper order of filing according to the Rules for Alphabetic Filing, given before, and the sample question given below. Print the letter of the correct answer in the space at the right.

SAMPLE QUESTION

Column I		Column II	
w.	Jane Earl	A.	w, y, z, x
x.	James A. Earle	B.	y, w, z, x
y.	James Earl	C.	x, y, w, z
z.	J. Earle	D.	x, w, y, z

The correct way to file the cards is:
- y. James Earl
- w. Jane Earl
- z. J. Earle
- x. James A. Earle

The correct filing order is shown by the letters, y, w, z, x (in that sequence). Since, in Column II, B appears in front of the letters, y, w, z, x (in that sequence), B is the correct answer to the sample question.

Now answer the following questions using that same procedure.

		Column I			Column II		
1.	w.	James Rothschild	A.	x, z, w, y			1.____
	x.	Julius B. Rothchild	B.	x, w, z, y			
	y.	B. Rothstein	C.	z, y, w, x			
	z.	Brian Joel Rothenstein	D.	z, w, x, y			
2.	w.	George S. Wise	A.	w, y, z, x			2.____
	x.	S. G. Wise	B.	x, w, y, z			
	y.	Geo. Stuart Wise	C.	y, x, w, z			
	z.	Prof. Diana Wise	D.	z, w, y, x			
3.	w.	10th Street Bus Terminal	A.	x, z, w, y			3.____
	x.	Buckingham Travel Agency	B.	y, x, w, z			
	y.	The Buckingham Theater	C.	w, z, y, x			
	z.	Burt Tompkins Studio	D.	x, w, y, z			
4.	w.	National Council of American Importers	A.	w, y, x, z			4.____
			B.	x, z, w, y			
	x.	National Chain Co. of Providence	C.	z, x, w, y			
	y.	National Council on Alcoholism	D.	z, x, y, w			
	z.	National Chain Co.					

5.   w.   Dr. Herbert Alvary   A.   w, y, x, z   5._____
       x.   Mr. Victor Alvarado   B.   z, w, x, y
       y.   Alvar Industries   C.   y, z, x, w
       z.   V. Alvarado   D.   w, z, x, y

6.   w.   Joan MacBride   A.   w, x, z, y   6._____
       x.   Wm. Mackey   B.   w, y, z, x
       y.   Roslyn McKenzie   C.   w, z, x, y
       z.   Winifred Mackey   D.   w, y, x, z

7.   w.   3 Way Trucking Co.   A.   y, x, z, w   7._____
       x.   3rd Street Bakery   B.   y, z, w, x
       y.   380 Realty Corp.   C.   x, y, z, w
       z.   Three Lions Pub   D.   x, y, w, z

8.   w.   Miss Rose Leonard   A.   z, w, x, y   8._____
       x.   Rev. Leonard Lucas   B.   w, z, y, x
       y.   Sylvia Leonard Linen Shop   C.   w, x, z, y
       z.   Rose S. Leonard   D.   z, w, y, x

KEY (CORRECT ANSWERS)

1.   A
2.   D
3.   B
4.   D
5.   C
6.   A
7.   C
8.   B

TEST 2

DIRECTIONS: Questions 1 through 7 each show in Column I four names (lettered w, x, y, z) which have to be entered in an agency telephone directory. You are to choose the option (lettered A, B, C, or D) in Column II which *BEST* represents the proper order for entering them according to the Rules for Alphabetic Filing, given before, and the sample question given below.

SAMPLE QUESTION

	Column I		Column II
w.	Doris Jenkin	A.	w, y, z, x
x.	Donald F. Jenkins	B.	y, w, z, x
y.	Donald Jenkin	C.	x, y, w, z
z.	D. Jenkins	D.	x, w, y, z

The correct way to enter these names is:

y.	Donald Jenkin
w.	Doris Jenkin
z.	D. Jenkins
x.	Donald F. Jenkins

The correct order is shown by the letters y, w, z, x, in that sequence. Since, in Column II, B appears in front of the letters y, w, z, x, in that sequence, B is the correct answer to the sample question.

Now answer the following questions using the same procedure.

		Column I		Column II	
1.	w.	Lawrence Robertson	A.	x, y, w, z	1._____
	x.	Jack L. Robinson	B.	w, z, x, y	
	y.	John Robinson	C.	z, w, x, y	
	z.	William B. Roberson	D.	z, w, y, x	
2.	w.	P. N. Figueredo	A.	y, x, z, w	2._____
	x.	M. Alice Figueroa	B.	x, z, w, y	
	y.	Jose Figueredo	C.	x, w, z, y	
	z.	M. Alicia Figueroa	D.	y, w, x, z	
3.	w.	George Steven Keats	A.	y, x, w, z	3._____
	x.	George S. Keats	B.	z, y, x, w	
	y.	G. Samuel Keats	C.	x, z, w, y	
	z.	Dr. Samuel Keats	D.	w, z, x, y	
4.	w.	V. Merchant	A.	w, x, y, z	4._____
	x.	Dr. William Mercher	B.	w, y, z, x	
	y.	Prof. Victor Merchant	C.	z, y, w, x	
	z.	Dr. Walter Merchan	D.	z, w, y, x	
5.	w.	Brian McCoy	A.	z, x, y, w	5._____
	x.	William Coyne	B.	y, w, z, x	
	y.	Mr. William MacCoyle	C.	x, z, y, w	
	z.	Dr. D. V. Coyne	D.	w, y, z, x	

6. w. Ms. M. Rosie Buchanan   A. z, y, x, w   6.____
    x. Rosalyn M. Buchanan   B. w, z, x, y
    y. Rosie Maria Buchanan   C. w, z, y, x
    z. Rosa Marie Buchanan   D. z, x, y, w

7. w. Prof. Jonathan Praga   A. w, z, y, x   7.____
    x. Dr. Joan Prager   B. w, x, z, y
    y. Alan VanPrague   C. x, w, z, y
    z. Alexander Prague   D. x, w, y, z

KEY (CORRECT ANSWERS)

1. C
2. D
3. A
4. D
5. A
6. B
7. B

TEST 3

DIRECTIONS: Questions 1 through 10 each show in Column I names written on four cards (lettered w, x, y, z) which have to be filed. You are to choose the option (lettered A, B, C, or D) in Column II which *BEST* represents the proper order of filing according to the rules and sample question given below. The cards are to be filed according to the Rules for Alphabetical Filing, given before, and the sample question given below.

SAMPLE QUESTION

	Column I		Column II
w.	Jane Earl	A.	w, y, z, x
x.	James A. Earle	B.	y, w, z, x
y.	James Earl	C.	x, y, w, z
z.	J. Earle	D.	x, w, y, z

The correct way to file the cards is:
- y. James Earl
- w. Jane Earl
- z. J. Earle
- x. James A. Earle

The correct filing order is shown by the letters y, w, z, x (in that order). Since, in Column II, B appears in front of the letters y, w, z, x (in that order), B is the correct answer to the sample question.

Now answer Questions 1 through 10 using the same procedure.

		Column I		Column II	
1.	w.	John Smith	A.	w, x, y, z	1.____
	x.	Joan Smythe	B.	y, z, x, w	
	y.	Gerald Schmidt	C.	y, z, w, x	
	z.	Gary Schmitt	D.	z, y, w, x	
2.	w.	A. Black	A.	w, x, y, z	2.____
	x.	Alan S. Black	B.	w, y, x, z	
	y.	Allan Black	C.	w, y, z, x	
	z.	Allen A. Black	D.	x, w, y, z	
3.	w.	Samuel Haynes	A.	w, x, y, z	3.____
	x.	Sam C. Haynes	B.	x, w, z, y	
	y.	David Haynes	C.	y, z, w, x	
	z.	Dave L. Haynes	D.	z, y, x, w	
4.	w.	Lisa B. McNeil	A.	x, y, w, z	4.____
	x.	Tom MacNeal	B.	x, z, y, w	
	y.	Lisa McNeil	C.	y, w, z, x	
	z.	Lorainne McNeal	D.	z, x, y, w	
5.	w.	Larry Richardson	A.	w, y, x, z	5.____
	x.	Leroy Richards	B.	y, x, z, w	
	y.	Larry S. Richards	C.	y, z, x, w	
	z.	Leroy C. Richards	D.	x, w, z, y	

6.	w.	Arlene Lane	A.	w, z, y, x	6._____
	x.	Arlene Cora Lane	B.	w, z, x, y	
	y.	Arlene Clair Lane	C.	y, x, z, w	
	z.	Arlene C. Lane	D.	z, y, w, x	

7.	w.	Betty Fish	A.	w, x, z, y	7._____
	x.	Prof. Ann Fish	B.	x, w, y, z	
	y.	Norma Fisch	C.	y, z, x, w	
	z.	Dr. Richard Fisch	D.	z, y, w, x	

8.	w.	Dr. Anthony David Lukak	A.	w, y, z, x	8._____
	x.	Mr. Steven Charles Lucas	B.	x, z, w, y	
	y.	Mr. Anthony J. Lukak	C.	z, x, y, w	
	z.	Prof. Steven C. Lucas	D.	z, x, w, y	

9.	w.	Martha Y. Lind	A.	w, y, z, x	9._____
	x.	Mary Beth Linden	B.	w, y, x, z	
	y.	Martha W. Lind	C.	y, w, z, x	
	z.	Mary Bertha Linden	D.	y, w, x, z	

10.	w.	Prof. Harry Michael MacPhelps	A.	w, z, x, y	10._____
	x.	Mr. Horace M. MacPherson	B.	w, y, z, x	
	y.	Mr. Harold M. McPhelps	C.	z, x, w, y	
	z.	Prof. Henry Martin MacPher-son	D.	x, z, y, w	

KEY (CORRECT ANSWERS)

1.	C	6.	A
2.	A	7.	C
3.	D	8.	D
4.	B	9.	C
5.	B	10.	A

TEST 4

DIRECTIONS: Answer Questions 1 through 5 on the basis of the following information:

A certain shop keeps an informational card file on all suppliers and merchandise. On each card is the supplier's name, the contract number for the merchandise he supplies, and a delivery date for the merchandise. In this filing system, the supplier's name is filed alphabetically, the contract number for the merchandise is filed numerically, and the delivery date is filed chronologically.
In Questions 1 through 5 there are five notations numbered 1 through 5 shown in Column I. Each notation is made up of a supplier's name, a contract number, and a date which is to be filed according to the following rules:

First: File in alphabetical order;
Second: When two or more notations have the same supplier, file according to the contract number in numerical order beginning with the lowest number;
Third: When two or more notations have the same supplier and contract number, file according to the date beginning with the earliest date.
In Column II the numbers 1 through 5 are arranged in four ways to show four different orders in which the merchandise information might
be filed. Pick th.e answer (A., B, C, or D) in Column II in which the notations are arranged according to the above filing rules.

SAMPLE QUESTION

Column I			Column II	
1.	Cluney (4865) 6/17/02		A.	2, 3, 4, 1, 5
2.	Roster (2466) 5/10/01		B.	2, 5, 1, 3, 4
3.	Altool (7114) 10/15/02		C.	3, 2, 1, 4, 5
4.	Cluney (5296) 12/18/01		D.	3, 5, 1, 4, 2
5.	Cluney (4865) 4/8/02			

The correct way to file the cards is:

3.	Altool (7114)	10/15/02
5.	Cluney (4865)	4/8/02
1.	Cluney (4865)	6/17/02
4.	Cluney (5276)	12/18/01
2.	Roster (2466)	5/10/01

Since the correct filing order is 3, 5, 1, 4, 2, the answer to the sample question is D. Now answer Questions 1 through 5.

		Column I				Column II	
1.	1.	warren	(96063)	3/30/03	A.	2, 4, 3, 5, 1
	2.	moore	(21237)	9/4/04	B.	2, 3, 5, 4, 1
	3.	newman	(10050)	12/12/03	C.	4, 5, 2, 3, 1
	4.	downs	(81251)	1/2/03	D.	4, 2, 3, 5, 1
	5.	oliver	(60145)	6/30/04		

1._____

2.	1.	Henry	(40552)	7/6/04	A.	5, 4, 3, 1, 2	2.___
	2.	Boyd	(91251)	9/1/03	B.	2, 3, 4, 1, 5	
	3.	George	(8196)	12/12/03	C.	2, 4, 3, 1, 5	
	4.	George	(31096)	1/12/04	D.	5, 2, 3, 1, 4	
	5.	West	(6109)	8/9/03			
3.	1.	Salba	(4670)	9/7/03	A.	5, 3, 1, 2, 4	3.___
	2.	Salba	(51219)	3/1/03	B.	3, 1, 2, 4, 5	
	3.	Crete	(81562)	7/1/04	C.	3, 5, 4, 2, 1	
	4.	Salba	(51219)	1/11/04	D.	5, 3, 4, 2, 1	
	5.	Texi	(31549)	1/25/03			
4.	1.	Crayone	(87105)	6/10/04	A.	1, 2, 5, 3, 4	4.___
	2.	Shamba	(49210)	1/5/03	B.	1, 5, 2, 3, 4	
	3.	Valiant	(3152)	5/1/04	C.	1, 5, 3, 4, 2	
	4.	Valiant	(3152)	1/9/04	D.	1, 5, 2, 4, 3	
	5.	Poro	(59613)	7/1/03			
5.	1.	Mackie	(42169)	12/20/03	A.	3, 2, 1, 5, 4	5.___
	2.	Lebo	(5198)	9/12/02	B.	3, 2, 4, 5, 1	
	3.	Drummon	(99631)	9/9/04	C.	3, 5, 2, 4, 1	
	4.	Lebo	(15311)	1/25/02	D.	3, 5, 4, 2, 1	
	5.	Harvin	(81765)	6/2/03			

KEY (CORRECT ANSWERS)

1. D
2. B
3. B
4. D
5. C

TEST 5

DIRECTIONS: Each of Questions 1 through 8 represents five cards to be filed, numbered 1 through 5 in Column I. Each card is made up of the employee's name, the date of a work assignment, and the work assignment code number shown in parentheses. The cards are to be filed according to the following rules:

First: File in alphabetical order;

Second: When two or more cards have the same employee's name, file according to the assignment date beginning with the earliest date;

Third: When two or more cards have the same employee's name and the same date, file according to the work assignment number beginning with the lowest number.

Column II shows the cards arranged in four different orders. Pick the answer (A, B, C, or D) in Column II which shows the cards arranged correctly according to the above filing rules.

SAMPLE QUESTION

	Column I				Column II
1.	Cluney	4/8/02	(486503)	A.	2, 3, 4, 1, 5
2.	Roster	5/10/01	(246611)	B.	2, 5, 1, 3, 4
3.	Altool	10/15/02	(711433)	C.	3, 2, 1, 4, 5
4.	Cluney	12/18/02	(527610)	D.	3, 5, 1, 4, 2
5.	Cluney	4/8/02	(486500)		

The correct way to file the cards is:
- 3.   Altool 10/15/02 (711433)
- 5.   Cluney 4/8/02 (486500)
- 1.   Cluney 4/8/02 (486503)
- 4.   Cluney 12/18/02 (527610)
- 2.   Roster 5/10/01 (246611)

The correct filing order is shown by the numbers in front of each name (3, 5, 1, 4, 2). The answer to the sample question is the letter in Column II in front of the numbers 3, 5, 1, 4, 2. This answer is D.

Now answer Questions 1 through 8 according to these rules.

		Column I				Column II	
1.	1.	Kohls	4/2/02	(125677)	A.	1, 2, 3, 4, 5	1._____
	2.	Keller	3/21/02	(129698)	B.	3, 2, 1, 4, 5	
	3.	Jackson	4/10/02	(213541)	C.	3, 1, 2, 4, 5	
	4.	Richards	1/9/03	(347236)	D.	5, 2, 1, 3, 4	
	5.	Richmond	12/11/01	(379321)			

		Column I				Column II	
2.	1.	Burroughs	5/27/02	(237896)	A.	1, 4, 3, 2, 5	2._____
	2.	Charlson	1/16/02	(114537)	B.	4, 1, 5, 3, 2	
	3.	Carlsen	12/2/02	(114377)	C.	1, 4, 3, 5, 2	
	4.	Burton	5/1/02	(227096)	D.	4, 1, 3, 5, 2	
	5.	Charlson	12/2/02	(114357)			

3.	A.	Ungerer	11/11/02	(537924)		A.	1, 5, 3, 2, 4		3.__
	B.	Winters	1/10/02	(657834)		B.	5, 1, 3, 4, 2		
	C.	Ventura	12/1/02	(698694)		C.	3, 5, 1, 2, 4		
	D.	Winters	10/11/02	(675654)		D.	1, 5, 3, 4, 2		
	E.	Ungaro	1/10/02	(684325)					
4.	1.	Norton	3/12/03	(071605)		A.	1, 4, 2, 3, 5		4.__
	2.	Morris	2/26/03	(068931)		B.	3, 5, 2, 4, 1		
	3.	Morse	5/12/03	(142358)		C.	2, 4, 3, 5, 1		
	4.	Morris	2/26/03	(068391)		D.	4, 2, 5, 3, 1		
	5.	Morse	2/26/03	(068391)					
5.	1.	Eger	4/19/02	(874129)		A.	3, 4, 1, 2, 5		5.__
	2.	Eihler	5/19/03	(875329)		B.	1, 4, 5, 2, 3		
	3.	Ehrlich	11/19/02	(874839)		C.	4, 1, 3, 2, 5		
	4.	Eger	4/19/02	(876129)		D.	1, 4, 3, 5, 2		
	5.	Eihler	5/19/02	(874239)					
6.	1.	Johnson	12/21/02	(786814)		A.	2, 4, 3, 5, 1		6.__
	2.	Johns	12/21/03	(801024)		B.	4, 2, 5, 3, 1		
	3.	Johnson	12/12/03	(762814)		C.	4, 5, 3, 1, 2		
	4.	Jackson	12/12/03	(862934)		D.	5, 3, 1, 2, 4		
	5.	Johnson	12/12/03	(762184)					
7.	1.	Fuller	7/12/02	(598310)		A.	2, 1, 5, 4, 3		7.__
	2.	Fuller	7/2/02	(598301)		B.	1, 2, 4, 5, 3		
	3.	Fuller	7/22/02	(598410)		C.	1, 4, 5, 2, 3		
	4.	Fuller	7/17/03	(598710)		D.	2, 1, 3, 5, 4		
	5.	Fuller	7/17/03	(598701)					
8.	1.	Perrine	10/27/99	(637096)		A.	3, 4, 5, 1, 2		8.__
	2.	Perrone	11/14/02	(767609)		B.	3, 2, 5, 4, 1		
	3.	Perrault	10/15/98	(629706)		C.	5, 3, 4, 1, 2		
	4.	Perrine	10/17/02	(373656)		D.	4, 5, 1, 2, 3		
	5.	Perine	10/17/01	(376356)					

KEY (CORRECT ANSWERS)

1. B
2. A
3. B
4. D
5. D
6. B
7. D
8. C

TEST 6

DIRECTIONS: Each question or incomplete statement is followed by several suggested answers or completions. Select the one that *BEST* answers the question or completes the statement. *PRINT THE LETTER OF THE CORRECT ANSWER IN THE SPACE AT THE RIGHT.*

1. Which one of the following *BEST* describes the usual arrangement of a tickler file?   1.____

   A. Alphabetical   B. Chronological
   C. Numerical   D. Geographical

2. Which one of the following is the *LEAST* desirable filing practice?   2.____

   A. Using staples to keep papers together
   B. Filing all material without regard to date
   C. Keeping a record of all materials removed from the files
   D. Writing filing instructions on each paper prior to filing

3. The one of the following records which it would be *MOST* advisable to keep in alphabetical order is a   3.____

   A. continuous listing of phone messages, including time and caller, for your supervisor
   B. listing of individuals currently employed by your agency in a particular title
   C. record of purchases paid for by the petty cash fund
   D. dated record of employees who have borrowed material from the files in your office

4. Tickler systems are used in many legal offices for scheduling and calendar control. Of the following, the *LEAST* common use of a tickler system is to   4.____

   A. keep papers filed in such a way that they may easily be retrieved
   B. arrange for the appearance of witnesses when they will be needed
   C. remind lawyers when certain papers are due
   D. arrange for the gathering of certain types of evidence

5. A type of file which permits the operator to remain seated while the file can be moved backward and forward as required is *BEST* termed a   5.____

   A. lateral file   B. movable file
   C. reciprocating file   D. rotary file

6. In which of the following cases would it be *MOST* desirable to have two cards for one individual in a single alphabetic file? The individual has   6.____

   A. a hyphenated surname
   B. two middle names
   C. a first name with an unusual spelling
   D. a compound first name

KEY (CORRECT ANSWERS)

1. B
2. B
3. B
4. A
5. C
6. A

———

SPELLING
EXAMINATION SECTION
TEST 1

DIRECTIONS: One word in each lettered group is misspelled. Indicate the letter of the misspelled word in the space at the right. Mark "E" if all are spelled correctly.

1.	A.	sacriligious	B.	ingenius	C.	advantageous	D.	ingenuous	1._____
2.	A.	apparrel	B.	barrel	C.	quarrel	D.	sorrel	2._____
3.	A.	carousal	B.	cannester	C.	carrousel	D.	cygnet	3._____
4.	A.	preliminary	B.	cemetary	C.	seminary	D.	eleemosynary	4._____
5.	A.	croquet	B.	kimono	C.	cocoanut	D.	carom	5._____
6.	A.	chattel	B.	privelege	C.	convenience	D.	immerse	6._____
7.	A.	resiliant	B.	aspirant	C.	adherent	D.	conversant	7._____
8.	A.	sacrilege	B.	entourage	C.	demurage	D.	persiflage	8._____
9.	A.	disappoint	B.	dissatisfy	C.	dessicate	D.	dissuade	9._____
10.	A.	fallacy	B.	fantasy	C.	ecstacy	D.	hypocrisy	10._____
11.	A.	elegible	B.	illegible	C.	intelligible	D.	irascible	11._____
12.	A.	emission	B.	omission	C.	incision	D.	comission	12._____
13.	A.	narrate	B.	exaggerrate	C.	disintegrate	D.	hyphenate	13._____
14.	A.	chagrined	B.	humbugged	C.	kidnapped	D.	fidgetted	14._____
15.	A.	flaccid	B.	succinct	C.	rancid	D.	accrid	15._____
16.	A.	forehead	B.	foresworn	C.	foresight	D.	forerunner	16._____
17.	A.	guard	B.	language	C.	guarantee	D.	guage	17._____
18.	A.	embarrassed	B.	harrassed	C.	terraced	D.	harnessed	18._____
19.	A.	persuade	B.	imperterbable	C.	pursuit	D.	purport	19._____
20.	A.	innuendo	B.	inoculate	C.	inovation	D.	innocuous	20._____
21.	A.	weird	B.	inviegle	C.	siege	D.	seized	21._____
22.	A.	ratify	B.	rarefy	C.	liquify	D.	ramify	22._____
23.	A.	muscles	B.	mussels	C.	missals	D.	missies	23._____
24.	A.	Philippines	B.	penicillen	C.	patrolling	D.	prairie	24._____
25.	A.	questionaire	B.	fanfare	C.	flair	D.	solitaire	25._____

KEY (CORRECT ANSWERS)

1.	A	sacrilegious
2.	A	apparel
3.	B	cannister
4.	B	cemetery
5.	E	
6.	B	privilege
7.	A	resilient
8.	C	demurrage
9.	C	desiccate
10.	C	ecstasy
11.	A	eligible
12.	D	commission
13.	B	exaggerate
14.	D	fidgeted
15.	D	acrid
16.	B	forsworn
17.	D	gauge
18.	B	harassed
19.	B	imperturbable
20.	C	innovation
21.	B	inveigle
22.	C	liquefy
23.	D	missiles
24.	B	penicillin
25.	A	questionnaire

———

TEST 2

DIRECTIONS: Two words in each lettered group are INCORRECTLY spelled. Indicate the two misspelled words in each group in the space at the right.

1.	A. accidently	B. apology	C. description	D. devide	1._____
2.	A. accomodate	B. apparatus	C. business	D. desireable	2._____
3.	A. arguement	B. conscience	C. dining	D. convience	3._____
4.	A. across	B. atheletics	C. changeable	D. dissapoint	4._____
5.	A. choose	B. disasterous	C. dissatisfied	D. courtecy	5._____
6.	A. all right	B. allready	C. almost	D. alltogether	6._____
7.	A. eighth	B. formerly	C. formaly	D. begining	7._____
8.	A. ninth	B. forty	C. embarrasment	D. ninty	8._____
9.	A. fourth	B. lose	C. noticable	D. enviroment	9._____
10.	A. grammer	B. irrelevent	C. weight	D. either	10._____
11.	A. familar	B. similiar	C. its	D. width	11._____
12.	A. occassionally	B. occurence	C. government	D. exceed	12._____
13.	A. labatory	B. necessary	C. outragous	D. paid	13._____
14.	A. dipthong	B. pamphlett	C. hoping	D. illegible	14._____
15.	A. beleive	B. concieve	C. quite	D. quiet	15._____
16.	A. benefited	B. preferable	C. wheather	D. grievious	16._____
17.	A. counterfeit	B. serviceable	C. conferance	D. confidentally	17._____
18.	A. quantity	B. quality	C. probally	D. libary	18._____
19.	A. recieve	B. decieve	C. perform	D. preferred	19._____
20.	A. reconize	B. seperate	C. truly	D. inter	20._____
21.	A. perfessor	B. useing	C. proceed	D. impede	21._____
22.	A. you're	B. it's	C. preceed	D. impeed	22._____
23.	A. possession	B. pursue	C. pursuade	D. religeous	23._____
24.	A. rhythm	B. schedule	C. repitition	D. usualy	24._____
25.	A. mileage	B. peaceable	C. minature	D. superintendant	25._____

KEY (CORRECT ANSWERS)

1.	A,D	accidentally, divide
2.	A,D	accommodate, desirable
3.	A,D	argument, convenience
4.	A,D	athletics, disappoint
5.	B,D	disastrous, courtesy
6.	B,D	already, altogether
7.	C,D	formally, beginning
8.	C,D	embarrassment, ninety
9.	C,D	noticeable, environment
10.	A,B	grammar, irrelevant
11.	A,B	familiar, similar
12.	A,B	occasionally, occurrence
13.	A,C	laboratory, outrageous
14.	A,B	diphthong, pamphlet
15.	A,B	believe, conceive
16.	C,D	whether, grievous
17.	C,D	conference, confidentially
18.	C,D	probably, library
19.	A,B	receive, deceive
20.	A,B	recognize, separate
21.	A,B	professor, using
22.	C,D	precede, impede
23.	C,D	persuade, religious
24.	C,D	repetition, usually
25.	C,D	miniature, superintendent

———

TEST 3

DIRECTIONS: Two words in each lettered group are INCORRECTLY spelled. Indicate the two misspelled words in each group in the space at the right.

1.   A. consolible   B. libel   C. inteligible   D. irascible   1.____
2.   A. beneficient   B. correlative   C. awful   D. offeng   2.____
3.   A. tractible   B. malleable   C. tracable   D. exchangeable   3.____
4.   A. inviegle   B. weird   C. seige   D. seized   4.____
5.   A. recommend   B. saccharine   C. dillemma   D. millenium   5.____
6.   A. dissipated   B. loneliness   C. incidently   D. corroberate   6.____
7.   A. advantageous B. ingenious   C. facetous   D. ingenous   7.____
8.   A. inoculate   B. innuendo   C. inovation   D. inocuous   8.____
9.   A. embarassed   B. harrassed   C. harnessed   D. terraced   9.____
10. A. monsignier   B. mayorality   C. saxophone   D. liquefied   10.____
11. A. caravansery   B. compulsary   C. anniversary   D. adversary   11.____
12. A. duteable   B. scurilous   C. beseech   D. catechized   12.____
13. A. exaggerate   B. narrate   C. disintigrate   D. hyphenate   13.____
14. A. ommission   B. emission   C. omnitient   D. commission   14.____
15. A. persuit   B. purser   C. imperterbable   D. purport   15.____
16. A. adherrent   B. conversant   C. resiliant   D. aspirant   16.____
17. A. mussels   B. missils   C. missles   D. muscles   17.____
18. A. palaver   B. deffer   C. profer   D. prefer   18.____
19. A. million   B. batallion   C. pavillion   D. stallion   19.____
20. A. inability   B. intelligibility C. elligibility   D. fallability   20.____
21. A. alottment   B. equipment   C. detrement   D. installment   21.____
22. A. foresworn   B. forehead   C. forsight   D. forerunner   22.____
23. A. guage   B. language   C. gaurantee   D. guard   23.____
24. A. sorel   B. apparrel   C. barrel   D. quarrel   24.____
25. A. questionaire B. flaire   C. fanfare   D. solitary   25.____

KEY (CORRECT ANSWERS)

1.	A,C	consolable, intelligible
2.	A,D	beneficent, offing
3.	A,C	tractable, traceable
4.	A,C	inveigle, siege
5.	C,D	dilemma, millennium
6.	C,D	incidentally, corroborate
7.	C,D	facetious, ingenious
8.	C,D	innovation, innocuous
9.	A,B	embarrassed, harassed
10.	A,B	monsignior, mayoralty
11.	A,B	caravansary, compulsory
12.	A,B	dutiable, scurrilous
13.	A,C	exaggerate, disintegrate
14.	A,C	omission, omniscient
15.	A,C	pursuit, imperturbable
16.	A,C	adherent, resilient
17.	B,C	missals, missiles
18.	B,C	defer, proffer
19.	B,C	battalion, pavilion
20.	C,D	eligibility, fallibility
21.	A,C	allotment, detriment
22.	A,C	forsworn, foresight
23.	A,C	gauge, guarantee
24.	A,B	sorrel, apparel
25.	A,B	questionnaire, flair

EXAMINATION SECTION
TEST 1

DIRECTIONS: Each question or incomplete statement is followed by several suggested answers or completions. Select the one that BEST answers the question or completes the statement. *PRINT THE LETTER OF THE CORRECT ANSWER IN THE SPACE AT THE RIGHT.*

1. Which of the following sentences is punctuated INCORRECTLY?   1._D_

    A. Johnson said, "One tiny virus, Blanche, can multiply so fast that it will become 200 viruses in 25 minutes."
    B. With economic pressures hitting them from all sides, American farmers have become the weak link in the food chain.
    C. The degree to which this is true, of course, depends on the personalities of the people involved, the subject matter, and the atmosphere in general.
    D. "What loneliness, asked George Eliot, is more lonely than distrust?"

2. Which of the following sentences is punctuated INCORRECTLY?   2._A_

    A. Based on past experiences, do you expect the plumber to show up late, not have the right parts, and overcharge you.
    B. When polled, however, the participants were most concerned that it be convenient.
    C. No one mentioned the flavor of the coffee, and no one seemed to care that china was used instead of plastic.
    D. As we said before, sometimes people view others as things; they don't see them as living, breathing beings like themselves.

3. Convention members travelled here from Kingston New York Pittsfield Massachusetts Bennington Vermont and Hartford Connecticut.
How many commas should there be in the above sentence?   3._A_ _B_

    A. 3   B. 4   C. 5   D. 6

4. Of the two speakers the one who spoke about human rights is more famous and more humble.
How many commas should there be in the above sentence?   4._A_

    A. 1   B. 2   C. 3   D. 4

5. Which sentence is punctuated INCORRECTLY?   5._B_ _B_

    A. Five people voted no; two voted yes; one person abstained.
    B. Well, consider what has been said here today, but we won't make any promises.
    C. Anthropologists divide history into three major periods: the Stone Age, the Bronze Age, and the Iron Age.
    D. Therefore, we may create a stereotype about people who are unsuccessful; we may see them as lazy, unintelligent, or afraid of success.

6. Which sentence is punctuated INCORRECTLY?   6._____

    A. Studies have found that the unpredictability of customer behavior can lead to a great deal of stress, particularly if the behavior is unpleasant or if the employee has little control over it.

B. If this degree of emotion and variation can occur in spectator sports, imagine the role that perceptions can play when there are <u>real</u> stakes involved.

C. At other times, however hidden expectations may sabotage or severely damage an encounter without anyone knowing what happened.

D. There are usually four issues to look for in a conflict: differences in values, goals, methods, and facts.

Questions 7-10.

DIRECTIONS: Questions 7 through 10 test your ability to distinguish between words that sound alike but are spelled differently and have different meanings. In the following groups of sentences, one of the underlined words is used incorrectly.

7. A. By accepting responsibility for their actions, managers promote trust.   7._____
    B. Dropping hints or making <u>illusions</u> to things that you would like changed sometimes leads to resentment.
    C. The entire unit <u>loses</u> respect for the manager and resents the reprimand.
    D. Many people are <u>averse</u> to confronting problems directly; they would rather avoid them.

8. A. What does this say about the <u>effect</u> our expectations have on those we supervise?   8._____
    B. In an effort to save time between 9 A.M. and 1 P.M., the staff members devised their own interpretation of what was to be done on these forms.
    C. The task master's <u>principal</u> concern is for getting the work done; he or she is not concerned about the needs or interests of employees.
    D. The advisor's main objective was increasing Angela's ability to invest her <u>capitol</u> wisely.

9. A. A typical problem is that people have to cope with the internal <u>censer</u> of their feelings.   9._____
    B. Sometimes, in their attempt to sound more learned, people speak in ways that are barely <u>comprehensible</u>.
    C. The <u>council</u> will meet next Friday to decide whether Abrams should continue as representative.
    D. His <u>descent</u> from grace was assured by that final word.

10. A. The doctor said that John's leg had to remain <u>stationary</u> or it would not heal properly.   10._____
    B. There is a city <u>ordinance</u> against parking too close to fire hydrants.
    C. Meyer's problem is that he is never <u>discrete</u> when talking about office politics.
    D. Mrs. Thatcher probably worked harder <u>than</u> any other British Prime Minister had ever worked.

Questions 11-20.

DIRECTIONS: For each of the following groups of sentences in Questions 11 through 20, select the sentence which is the BEST example of English usage and grammar.

11. A. She is a woman who, at age sixty, is distinctly attractive and cares about how they look.
    B. It was a seemingly impossible search, and no one knew the problems better than she.
    C. On the surface, they are all sweetness and light, but his morbid character is under it.
    D. The minicopier, designed to appeal to those who do business on the run like architects in the field or business travelers, weigh about four pounds.

11.____

12. A. Neither the administrators nor the union representa- tive regret the decision to settle the disagreement.
    B. The plans which are made earlier this year were no longer being considered.
    C. I would have rode with him if I had known he was leaving at five.
    D. I don't know who she said had it.

12.____

13. A. Writing at a desk, the memo was handed to her for immediate attention.
    B. Carla didn't water Carl's plants this week, which she never does.
    C. Not only are they good workers, with excellent writing and speaking skills, and they get to the crux of any problem we hand them.
    D. We've noticed that this enthusiasm for undertaking new projects sometimes interferes with his attention to detail.

13.____

14. A. It's obvious that Nick offends people by being unruly, inattentive, and having no patience.
    B. Marcia told Genie that she would have to leave soon.
    C. Here are the papers you need to complete your investigation.
    D. Julio was startled by you're comment.

14.____

15. A. The new manager has done good since receiving her promotion, but her secretary has helped her a great deal.
    B. One of the personnel managers approached John and tells him that the client arrived unexpectedly.
    C. If somebody can supply us with the correct figures, they should do so immediately.
    D. Like zealots, advocates seek power because they want to influence the policies and actions of an organization .

15.____

16. A. Between you and me, Chris probably won't finish this assignment in time.
    B. Rounding the corner, the snack bar appeared before us.
    C. Parker's radical reputation made to the Supreme Court his appointment impossible.
    D. By the time we arrived, Marion finishes briefing James and returns to Hank's office.

16.____

17.   A. As we pointed out earlier, the critical determinant of the success of middle manag-   17._____
ers is their ability to communicate well with others.
      B. The lecturer stated there wasn't no reason for bad supervision.
      C. We are well aware whose at fault in this instance.
      D. When planning important changes, it's often wise to seek the partic-
ipation of others because employees often have much valuable
ideas to offer.

18.   A. Joan had ought to throw out those old things that were damaged when the roof   18._____
leaked.
      B. I spose he'll let us know what he's decided when he finally comes to
a decision.
      C. Carmen was walking to work when she suddenly realized that she
had left her lunch on the table as she passed the market.
      D. Are these enough plants for your new office?

19.   A. First move the lever forward, and then they should lift the ribbon casing before try-   19._____
ing to take it out.
      B. Michael finished quickest than any other person in the office.
      C. There is a special meeting for we committee members today at 4
p.m.
      D. My husband is worried about our having to work overtime next
week.

20.   A. Another source of conflicts are individuals who possess very poor interpersonal   20._____
skills.
      B. It is difficult for us to work with him on projects because these kinds
of people are not interested in team building.
      C. Each of the departments was represented at the meeting.
      D. Poor boy, he never should of past that truck on the right.

Questions 21-28.

DIRECTIONS: In Questions 21 through 28, there may be a problem with English grammar or
usage. If a problem does exist, select the letter that indicates the most effective change. If no problem exists, select choice A.

21.   He rushed her to the hospital and stayed with her, even though this took quite a bit of his   21._____
time, he didn't charge her anything.

      A. No changes are necessary
      B. Change even though to although
      C. Change the first comma to a period and capitalize even
      D. Change rushed to had rushed

22.   Waiting that appears unfairly feels longer than waiting that seems justified.   22._____

      A. No changes are necessary
      B. Change unfairly to unfair
      C. Change appears to seems
      D. Change longer to longest

23. May be you and the person who argued with you will be able to reach an agreement.　23.____

    A. No changes are necessary
    B. Change will be to were
    C. Change argued with to had an argument with
    D. Change may be to maybe

24. Any one of them could of taken the file while you were having coffee.　24.____

    A. No changes are necessary
    B. Change any one to anyone
    C. Change of to have
    D. Change were having to were out having

25. While people get jobs or move from poverty level to better paying employment, they stop receiving benefits and start paying taxes.　25.____

    A. No changes are necessary
    B. Change While to As
    C. Change stop to will stop
    D. Change get to obtain

26. Maribeth's phone rang while talking to George about the possibility of their meeting Tom at three this afternoon.　26.____

    A. No changes are necessary
    B. Change their to her
    C. Move to George so that it follows Tom
    D. Change talking to she was talking

27. According to their father, Lisa is smarter than Chris, but Emily is the smartest of the three sisters.　27.____

    A. No changes are necessary
    B. Change their to her
    C. Change is to was
    D. Make two sentences, changing the second comma to a period and omitting but

28. Yesterday, Mark and he claim that Carl took Carol's ideas and used them inappropriately.　28.____

    A. No changes are necessary
    B. Change claim to claimed
    C. Change inappropriately to inappropriate
    D. Change Carol's to Carols'

Questions 29-34.

DIRECTIONS:　For each group of sentences in Questions 29 through 34, select the choice that represents the BEST editing of the problem sentence.

29. The managers expected employees to be at their desks at all times, but they would always be late or leave unannounced.　29.____

A. The managers wanted employees to always be at their desks, but they would always be late or leave unannounced.
B. Although the managers expected employees to be at their desks no matter what came up, they would always be late and leave without telling anyone.
C. Although the managers expected employees to be at their desks at all times, the managers would always be late or leave without telling anyone.
D. The managers expected the employee to never leave their desks, but they would always be late or leave without telling anyone.

30. The one who is department manager he will call you to discuss the problem tomorrow morning at 10 A.M.   30.____

   A. The one who is department manager will call you tomorrow morning at ten to discuss the problem.
   B. The department manager will call you to discuss the problem tomorrow at 10 A.M.
   C. Tomorrow morning at 10 A.M., the department manager will call you to discuss the problem.
   D. Tomorrow morning the department manager will call you to discuss the problem.

31. A conference on child care in the workplace the $200 cost of which to attend may be prohibitive to childcare workers who earn less than that weekly.   31.____

   A. A conference on child care in the workplace that costs $200 may be too expensive for childcare workers who earn less than that each week.
   B. A conference on child care in the workplace, the cost of which to attend is $200, may be prohibitive to childcare workers who earn less than that weekly.
   C. A conference on child care in the workplace who costs $200 may be too expensive for childcare workers who earn less than that a week.
   D. A conference on child care in the workplace which costs $200 may be too expensive to childcare workers who earn less than that on a weekly basis.

32. In accordance with estimates recently made, there are 40,000 to 50,000 nuclear weapons in our world today.   32.____

   A. Because of estimates recently, there are 40,000 to 50,000 nuclear weapons in the world today.
   B. In accordance with estimates made recently, there are 40,000 to 50,000 nuclear weapons in the world today.
   C. According to estimates made recently, there are 40,000 to 50,000 weapons in the world today.
   D. According to recent estimates, there are 40,000 to 50,000 nuclear weapons in the world today.

33. Motivation is important in problem solving, but they say that excessive motivation can inhibit the creative process.   33.____

   A. Motivation is important in problem solving, but, as they say, too much of it can inhibit the creative process.
   B. Motivation is important in problem solving and excessive motivation will inhibit the creative process.
   C. Motivation is important in problem solving, but excessive motivation can inhibit the creative process.

D. Motivation is important in problem solving because excessive motivation can inhibit the creative process.

34. In selecting the best option calls for consulting with all the people that are involved in it.   34.____

    A. In selecting the best option consulting with all the people concerned with it.
    B. Calling for the best option, we consulted all the affected people.
    C. We called all the people involved to select the best option.
    D. To be sure of selecting the best option, one should consult all the people involved.

35. There are a number of problems with the following letter. From the options below, select   35.____
the version that is MOST in accordance with standard business style, tone, and form.

Dear Sir:

We are so sorry that we have had to backorder your order for 15,000 widgets and 2,300 whatzits for such a long time. We have been having incredibly bad luck lately. When your order first came in no one could get to it because my secretary was out with the flu and her replacement didn't know what she was doing, then there was the dock strike in Cucamonga which held things up for awhile, and then it just somehow got lost. We think it may have fallen behind the radiator.

We are happy to say that all these problems have been taken care of, we are caught up on supplies, and we should have the stuff to you soon, in the near future --about two weeks. You may not believe us after everything you've been through with us, but it's true.

We'll let you know as soon as we have a secure date for delivery. Thank you so much for continuing to do business with us after all the problems this probably has caused you.

Yours very sincerely,

Rob Barker

    A. Dear Sir:

    We are so sorry that we have had to backorder your order for 15,000 widgets and 2,300 whatzits. We have been having problems with staff lately and the dock strike hasn't helped anything.

    We are happy to say that all these problems have been taken care of. I've told my secretary to get right on it, and we should have the stuff to you soon. Thank you so much for continuing to do business with us after all the problems this must have caused you.

    We'll let you know as soon as we have a secure date for delivery.

    Sincerely,

    Rob Barker

B.   Dear Sir:

We regret that we haven't been able to fill your order for 15,000 widgets and 2,300 whatzits in a timely fashion.

We'll let you know as soon as we have a secure date for delivery.

Sincerely,

Rob Barker

C.   Dear Sir:

We are so very sorry that we haven't been able to fill your order for 15,000 widgets and 2,300 whatzits. We have been having incredibly bad luck lately, but things are much better now.

Thank you so much for bearing with us through all of this. We'll let you know as soon as we have a secure date for delivery.

Sincerely,

Rob Barker

D.   Dear Sir:

We are very sorry that we haven't been able to fill your order for 15,000 widgets and 2,300 whatzits. Due to unforeseen difficulties, we have had to back-order your request. At this time, supplies have caught up to demand, and we foresee a delivery date within the next two weeks.

We'll let you know as soon as we have a secure date for delivery. Thank you for your patience.

Sincerely,

Rob Barker

———

KEY (CORRECT ANSWERS)

1.	D		16.	A
2.	A		17.	A
3.	B		18.	D
4.	A		19.	D
5.	B		20.	C
6.	C		21.	C
7.	B		22.	B
8.	D		23.	D
9.	A		24.	C
10.	C		25.	B
11.	B		26.	D
12.	D		27.	A
13.	D		28.	B
14.	C		29.	C
15.	D		30.	B

31.	A
32.	D
33.	C
34.	D
35.	D

ANSWER SHEET

TEST NO. _____ PART _____ TITLE OF POSITION _____

(AS GIVEN IN EXAMINATION ANNOUNCEMENT - INCLUDE OPTION, IF ANY)

PLACE OF EXAMINATION _____ DATE _____
(CITY OR TOWN)   (STATE)

RATING

USE THE SPECIAL PENCIL.   MAKE GLOSSY BLACK MARKS.

	A B C D E		A B C D E		A B C D E		A B C D E		A B C D E
1		26		51		76		101	
2		27		52		77		102	
3		28		53		78		103	
4		29		54		79		104	
5		30		55		80		105	
6		31		56		81		106	
7		32		57		82		107	
8		33		58		83		108	
9		34		59		84		109	
10		35		60		85		110	

Make only ONE mark for each answer.   Additional and stray marks may be
counted as mistakes.   In making corrections, erase errors COMPLETELY.

	A B C D E		A B C D E		A B C D E		A B C D E		A B C D E
11		36		61		86		111	
12		37		62		87		112	
13		38		63		88		113	
14		39		64		89		114	
15		40		65		90		115	
16		41		66		91		116	
17		42		67		92		117	
18		43		68		93		118	
19		44		69		94		119	
20		45		70		95		120	
21		46		71		96		121	
22		47		72		97		122	
23		48		73		98		123	
24		49		74		99		124	
25		50		75		100		125	

ANSWER SHEET

TEST NO. ______________ PART ______ TITLE OF POSITION ______________________________________
(AS GIVEN IN EXAMINATION ANNOUNCEMENT - INCLUDE OPTION, IF ANY)

PLACE OF EXAMINATION ______________________________ (CITY OR TOWN) ______________ (STATE) DATE ______________

RATING

USE THE SPECIAL PENCIL. MAKE GLOSSY BLACK MARKS.

1	A B C D E	26	A B C D E	51	A B C D E	76	A B C D E	101	A B C D E
2	A B C D E	27	A B C D E	52	A B C D E	77	A B C D E	102	A B C D E
3	A B C D E	28	A B C D E	53	A B C D E	78	A B C D E	103	A B C D E
4	A B C D E	29	A B C D E	54	A B C D E	79	A B C D E	104	A B C D E
5	A B C D E	30	A B C D E	55	A B C D E	80	A B C D E	105	A B C D E
6	A B C D E	31	A B C D E	56	A B C D E	81	A B C D E	106	A B C D E
7	A B C D E	32	A B C D E	57	A B C D E	82	A B C D E	107	A B C D E
8	A B C D E	33	A B C D E	58	A B C D E	83	A B C D E	108	A B C D E
9	A B C D E	34	A B C D E	59	A B C D E	84	A B C D E	109	A B C D E
10	A B C D E	35	A B C D E	60	A B C D E	85	A B C D E	110	A B C D E

Make only ONE mark for each answer. Additional and stray marks may be counted as mistakes. In making corrections, erase errors COMPLETELY.

11	A B C D E	36	A B C D E	61	A B C D E	86	A B C D E	111	A B C D E
12	A B C D E	37	A B C D E	62	A B C D E	87	A B C D E	112	A B C D E
13	A B C D E	38	A B C D E	63	A B C D E	88	A B C D E	113	A B C D E
14	A B C D E	39	A B C D E	64	A B C D E	89	A B C D E	114	A B C D E
15	A B C D E	40	A B C D E	65	A B C D E	90	A B C D E	115	A B C D E
16	A B C D E	41	A B C D E	66	A B C D E	91	A B C D E	116	A B C D E
17	A B C D E	42	A B C D E	67	A B C D E	92	A B C D E	117	A B C D E
18	A B C D E	43	A B C D E	68	A B C D E	93	A B C D E	118	A B C D E
19	A B C D E	44	A B C D E	69	A B C D E	94	A B C D E	119	A B C D E
20	A B C D E	45	A B C D E	70	A B C D E	95	A B C D E	120	A B C D E
21	A B C D E	46	A B C D E	71	A B C D E	96	A B C D E	121	A B C D E
22	A B C D E	47	A B C D E	72	A B C D E	97	A B C D E	122	A B C D E
23	A B C D E	48	A B C D E	73	A B C D E	98	A B C D E	123	A B C D E
24	A B C D E	49	A B C D E	74	A B C D E	99	A B C D E	124	A B C D E
25	A B C D E	50	A B C D E	75	A B C D E	100	A B C D E	125	A B C D E